COLLECTED POEMS

Michael Longley

CAPE POETRY

Published by Jonathan Cape 2006

2 4 6 8 10 9 7 5 3 1

First published in Great Britain in 2006 by
Jonathan Cape
Random House, 20 Vauxhall Bridge Road, London SW1V 2SA

Random House Australia (Pty) Limited
20 Alfred Street, Milsons Point, Sydney,
New South Wales 2061, Australia

Random House New Zealand Limited
18 Poland Road, Glenfield,
Auckland 10, New Zealand

Random House (Pty) Limited
Isle of Houghton, Corner of Boundary Road & Carse O'Gowrie,
Houghton, 2198, South Africa

The Random House Group Limited Reg. No. 954009
www.randomhouse.co.uk

A CIP catalogue record for this book is available from the British Library

ISBN 9780224080446

Papers used by Random House are natural,
recyclable products made from wood grown in sustainable forests.
The manufacturing processes conform to the environmental
regulations of the country of origin

Typeset by Palimpsest Book Production Limited, Polmont, Stirlingshire
Printed and bound in Great Britain by William Clowes Ltd, Beccles, Suffolk

COLLECTED POEMS

AUTHOR'S NOTE

Collected Poems includes all but nine of the poems in my eight volumes: *No Continuing City* (1969), *An Exploded View* (1973), *Man Lying on a Wall* (1976), *The Echo Gate* (1979), *Gorse Fires* (1991), *The Ghost Orchid* (1996), *The Weather in Japan* (2000) and *Snow Water* (2004). *Poems 1963-1983* contained the first four volumes and ended with *New Poems*, now Section V in this book. By and large I prefer not to tinker with past efforts: this resembles denting cold metal that was red-hot in another life. I have excised stanzas from four poems, and altered a very few titles. Some lines from two of the discarded pieces have been reworked elsewhere. I have added two new poems as an epilogue.

My first editor was Kevin Crossley-Holland, at Macmillan and then at Gollancz. Helen Owen looked after me at Secker & Warburg. Working on *Poems 1963-1983* with Tom Fenton of Salamander Press, discussing with him every aspect of the typeface, paper and binding, was an extraordinary experience. Peter Fallon of Gallery Press took the handsome result under his wing in Ireland. Robin Robertson has been my editor, at Secker & Warburg and Jonathan Cape, for nearly twenty years, attending the births of my last four collections and *Selected Poems*. I am very grateful to him, to my earlier editors, and to Dillon Johnston of Wake Forest University Press in North Carolina, my American publishers.

I dedicated *Poems 1963-1983* to the memory of my friends, Brian O'Donnell, carpenter and mender of musical instruments, who in the 1970s opened up for me the world of Irish traditional music; and Martin McBirney, polymath and deeply liberal QC and magistrate, who was murdered by the IRA in September 1974. These two men still represent for me a new Ireland. I have moved their dedicatory poem to p. 162 under the title 'A Last One'. I dedicated

Selected Poems (1998) to Eamonn Hughes and Bob Purdie who were brilliantly outspoken in their friendship at a time when true friends were needed:

> *When all the reeds are swaying in the wind*
> *How can you tell which reeds the otters bend?*

M.L.

CONTENTS

I
No Continuing City 1969

II

An Exploded View 1973

III

Man Lying on a Wall 1976

IV
The Echo Gate 1979

V

Poems 1985

VI
Gorse Fires 1991

VII
The Ghost Orchid 1995

VIII

The Weather in Japan 2000

IX
Snow Water 2004

X
Two New Poems

I

NO CONTINUING CITY
(1969)

for Edna

First dizzy cigarettes,
Tightlipped kisses,
Friendships, flying visits,
Birthdays, best wishes —

My children and my dead
Coming of age
In the turn of your head
As you turn a page.

For here we have no continuing city . . .

EPITHALAMION

These are the small hours when
Moths by their fatal appetite
That brings them tapping to get in,
   Are steered along the night
To where our window catches light.

   Who hazard all to be
Where we, the only two it seems,
Inhabit so delightfully
   A room it bursts its seams
And spills on to the lawn in beams,

   Such visitors as these
Reflect with eyes like frantic stars
This garden's brightest properties,
   Cruising its corridors
Of light above the folded flowers,

   Till our vicinity
Is rendered royal by their flight
Towards us, till more silently
   The silent stars ignite,
Their aeons dwindling by a night,

   And everything seems bent
On robing in this evening you
And me, all dark the element
   Our light is earnest to,
All quiet gathered round us who,

   When over the embankments
A train that's loudly reprobate
Shoots from silence into silence,
   With ease accommodate
Its pandemonium, its freight.

3

I hold you close because
We have decided dark will be
For ever like this and because,
    My love, already
The dark is growing elderly.

    With dawn upon its way,
Punctually and as a rule,
The small hours widening into day,
    Our room its vestibule
Before it fills all houses full,

    We too must hazard all,
Switch off the lamp without a word
For the last of night assembled
    Over it and unperturbed
By the moth that lies there littered,

    And notice how the trees
Which took on anonymity
Are again in their huge histories
    Displayed, that wherever we
Attempt, and as far as we can see,

    The flowers everywhere
Are withering, the stars dissolved,
Amalgamated in a glare,
    Which last night were revolved
Discreetly round us – and, involved,

    The two of us, in these
Which early morning has deformed,
Must hope that in new properties
    We'll find a uniform
To know each other truly by, or,

At the least, that these will,
When we rise, be seen with dawn
As remnant yet part raiment still,
  Like flags that linger on
The sky when king and queen are gone.

EMILY DICKINSON

Emily Dickinson, I think of you
Wakening early each morning to write,
Dressing with care for the act of poetry.
Yours is always a perfect progress through
Such cluttered rooms to eloquence, delight,
To words – your window on the mystery.

In your house in Amherst Massachusetts,
Though like love letters you lock them away,
The poems are ubiquitous as dust.
You sit there writing while the light permits –
While you grow older they increase each day,
Gradual as flowers, gradual as rust.

A QUESTIONNAIRE
FOR WALTER MITTY

for Harry Chambers

The opus virtuoso, the piano grand –
And how your unaccomplished fists extend
Themselves to musically athletic hands!

Mitty, on such voyages to legend
What luggage do you take? what currency?
Could it be truth you carry? lies you spend?

To climb an Everest or swim a sea –
No matter what the end in view – requires
A proper change of heart, some urgency.

In mixing with the doers and the triers
Whose dreaming modulates to enterprise,
Whose actions carry weight, whose churches spires,

Do you employ deceit or just disguise?
As agent, cipher or as catalyst
Do you conceal, do you apotheosise

These jungle pioneers, these pianists,
Your coinhabitants of wonderland,
Each one a namesake on the honours list?

At which side of the glass does Mitty stand
In his epiphany – in front? behind?
Or both – the hero with the also-ran?

And, Walter Mitty, how would you define
The water-walker who made the water wine –
Was it Christ the God? was it Christ the Man?

GRAFFITI

It would be painful, tedious and late
To alter awkward monsters such as these
To charming princes – metamorphoses
That all good fairy tales accelerate –

One kiss and, in the twinkling of an eye,
The Calibans accepted, warts and all,
At long last resurrected from the sty,
So blond, so beautiful, and six feet tall.

Through billboard forests, mists of lingerie,
These track a princess unequipped to change
Herself or them: her hair no winds derange,
Her thighs are locked, her cleavage legendary.

Lips where large allure but no response is,
Her all too perfect body they endure
By pencilling these bouquets of moustaches
As love's own emblem, their own signature.

Despite an aura vast enough to toss
Her neon constellations through the land,
She, in a realm too fragile to withstand
A single hair that is superfluous,

In paper palaces lies wintering,
While these who decorate her lovely crotch
With pubic shrubbery and with a notch,
Unwittingly imply a sort of spring. –

Such passion thwarted, such artistry released!
O where would Beauty be without her Beast?

THE ORNITHOLOGICAL
SECTION

in memory of John Harvey

Birds, such heavenly bric-à-brac
Without their guts, without their fears,
Despite the vital parts they lack
Have here maintained their proper cloth,
Have held their equilibrium
So perfectly, so many years,
Shed nothing but momentum,
Their only weather dust and moth.

Toward what feats and feasts they steer,
Toward what continents migrate,
Or simply why they disappear,
With feathers talons beaks and plumes
Kingfisher kestrel dodo swan
In life, in death can illustrate,
For ornithology keep on
Their uniforms, their best costumes.

In this unnatural treasury,
Though held thus by their own décors
And fixed in frozen augury,
Out of the past they dart and wade,
In such different skies to figure,
On so many half-remembered shores,
And are heading for the future,
By some deep need of ours conveyed.

Who quit their gay trajectories
Too suddenly, too long ago,
True to their movements, even these
Across our field of vision spill
And, while winging it through fable,
Fuse all we hope with what we know –
Their fate incontrovertible,
Their vanished bodies flying still.

We, with our histories left to spend,
Would have our actions thus defined
By that repose in which they end,
Would have these birds, these lively dead,
Who hesitate before they go
For ever out of sight and mind,
Whose long delays concern us so,
As our biographers instead.

We come as ornithologists –
As taxidermists we depart,
For here an urge we have persists
To recognise the tattered skins,
The bones come in at last to land
Of birds, entitled from the start,
Who take their places, make their stand
Where science ends and love begins.

CAMOUFLAGE

Our towns decayed, our gardens overgrown,
Weather we lament, the ivy creeping –
No matter what the setting, we are shown
(Whose one peculiar knack is weeping)
To differ from the beasts because they own
Those landscapes with which they are in keeping.

The leopard's coat accepting light through leaves,
Giraffes whose necks presume that certain trees
Are tall, whose elongated stance relieves
Those boughs of height's responsibilities –
Such attributes a balanced world conceives,
Itself reflected, its streams reflecting these.

We'd say they choose a mood to linger at:
Like white for weddings, black for funerals,
It turns to habit – then to habitat,
So deftly not a single one recalls
What he's exemplar of: more likely that
One long enlightened dawn these animals,

Betrayed by awkward mornings for an age,
By their furs and feathers long forsaken,
Put the usual scenery to advantage
But are nonetheless obliged to waken
(Amid the sanctuary of camouflage)
To a change of colour, a risk taken.

A PERSONAL STATEMENT

for Seamus Heaney

Since you, Mind, think to diagnose
        Experience
As summer, satin, nightingale or rose,
        Of the senses making sense –
            Follow my nose,

Attend all other points of contact,
        Deserve your berth:
My brain-child, help me find my own way back
        To fire, air, water, earth.
            I am, in fact,

More than a bag of skin and bone.
        My person is
A chamber where the elements postpone
        In lively synthesis,
            In peace on loan,

Old wars of flood and earthquake, storm
        And holocaust,
Their attributes most temperately reformed
        Of heatwave and of frost.
            They take my form,

Learn from my arteries their pace –
        They leave alarms
And excursions for my heart and lungs to face.
        I hold them in my arms
            And keep in place.

To walk, to run, to leap, to stand —
Of the litany
Of movement I the vicar in command,
The prophet in my country,
The priest at hand,

Take steps to make it understood
The occupants
Assembled here in narrow neighbourhood
Are my constituents
For bad or good.

Body and Mind, I turn to you.
It's me you fit.
Whatever you think, whatever you do,
Include me in on it,
Essential Two.

Who house philosophy and force,
Wed well in me
The elements, for fever's their divorce,
Nightmare and ecstasy,
And death of course.

My sponsor, Mind, my satellite,
Keep my balance,
Steer me through my heyday, through my night,
My senses' common sense,
Selfcentred light.

And you who set me in my ways,
Immaculate,
In full possession of my faculties —
Till you disintegrate,
Exist to please.

Lest I with fears and hopes capsize,
By your own lights
Sail, Body, cargoless towards surprise.
And come, Mind, raise your sights –
Believe my eyes.

THE OSPREY

To whom certain water talents –
Webbed feet, oils – do not occur,
Regulates his liquid acre
From the sky, his proper element.

There, already, his eye removes
The trout each fathom magnifies.
He lives, without compromise,
His unamphibious two lives –

An inextinguishable bird whom
No lake's waters waterlog.
He shakes his feathers like a dog.
It's all of air that ferries him.

ODYSSEY

Amateur witches and professional virgins,
Sirens and shepherdesses – all new areas
Of experience (I have been out of touch) –
Ladies, you are so many and various
You will have to put up with me, for your sins,
A stranger to your islands who knows too much.

Your coy advertisements for bed and breakfast
I take as read, if I feel inclined –
So easy-going am I through going steady
(Your photographs will never hang in my mind)
With one ear cocked for the weather forecast
I come ashore to you who remind me,

And, going out of my way to take a rest,
From sea sickness and the sea recuperate,
The sad fleets of capsized skulls behind me
And the wide garden they decorate.
Grant me anchorage as your paying guest –
Landladies, I have been too long at sea.

When I sight you playing ball on the sand,
A suggestion of hair under your arms,
Or, in shallows, wearing only the waves,
I unpack strictly avuncular charms –
To lose these sea legs I walk on land:
I linger till my boat fills up with leaves,

With snow or sunshine (whichever I prefer).
I see your islands as the residue
Of my sailor days, of this life afloat,
My lonely motive to abandon you,
Darlings, after each whirlwind love affair
Becalmed in logbook and in anecdote.

You have kept me going, despite delays –
On these devious shores where we coincide
I have never once outstayed my welcome
Though you all seem last resorts, my brides –
Your faces favourite landmarks always,
Your bodies comprising the long way home.

NAUSICAA

You scarcely raise a finger to the tide.
Pavilions, those days-off at the seaside

Collapse about your infinite arrest –
He sees your cove more clearly than the rest.

All evidence of dry land he relearns.
The ocean gathers where your shoulder turns.

NO CONTINUING CITY

My hands here, gentle, where her breasts begin,
My picture in her eyes –
It is time for me to recognise
This new dimension, my last girl.
So, to set my house in order, I imagine
Photographs, advertisements – the old lies,
The lumber of my soul –

All that is due for spring cleaning,
Everything that soul-destroys.
Into the open I bring
Girls who linger still in photostat
(For whom I was so many different boys) –
I explode their myths before it is too late,
Their promises I detonate –

There is quite a lot that I can do . . .
I leave them – are they six or seven, two or three? –
Locked in their small geographies.
The hillocks of their bodies' lovely shires
(Whose all weathers I have walked through)
Acre by acre recede entire
To summer country.

From collision to eclipse their case is closed.
Who took me by surprise
Like comets first – now, failing to ignite,
They constellate such uneventful skies,
Their stars arranged each night
In the old stories
Which I successfully have diagnosed.

Though they momentarily survive
In my delays,
They neither cancel nor improve
My continuing city with old ways,
Familiar avenues to love –
Down my one-way streets (it is time to finish)
Their eager syllables diminish.

Though they call out from the suburbs
Of experience – they know how that disturbs! –
Or, already tending towards home,
Prepare to hitch-hike on the kerbs,
Their bags full of dear untruths –
I am their medium
And I take the words out of their mouths.

From today new hoardings crowd my eyes,
Pasted over my ancient histories
Which (I must be cruel to be kind)
Only gale or cloudburst now discover,
Ripping the billboard of my mind –
Oh, there my lovers,
There my dead no longer advertise.

I transmit from the heart a closing broadcast
To my girl, my bride, my wife-to-be –
I tell her she is welcome,
Advising her to make this last,
To be sure of finding room in me
(I embody bed and breakfast) –
To eat and drink me out of house and home.

CIRCE

The cries of the shipwrecked enter my head.
On wildest nights when the torn sky confides
Its face to the sea's cracked mirror, my bed
– Addressed by the moon and her tutored tides –

Through brainstorm, through nightmare and ocean
Keeps me afloat. Shallows are my coven,
The comfortable margins – in this notion
I stand uncorrected by the sun even.

Out of the night husband after husband
– Eyes wide as oysters, arms full of driftwood –
Wades ashore and puts in at my island.
My necklaces of sea shells and seaweed,

My skirts of spindrift, sandals of flotsam
Catch the eye of each bridegroom for ever.
Quite forgetful of the widowing calm
My sailors wait through bad and good weather.

At first in rock pools I become their wife,
Under the dunes at last they lie with me –
These are the spring and neap tides of their life.
I have helped so many sailors off the sea,

And, counting no man among my losses,
I have made of my arms and my thighs last rooms
For the irretrievable and capsized –
I extend the sea, its idioms.

NARCISSUS

Unweatherbeaten as the moon my face
Among the waterlogged, the commonplace,

Old boots and kettles for inheritance
Drifting into my head on the off-chance –

A wide Sargasso where the names of things
(Important guests at all such christenings)

Submerge in mind and pool like treasure-trove.
My face as sole survivor floats above.

FREEZE-UP

The freeze-up annexes the sea even,
Putting out over the waves its platform.
Let skies fall, the fox's belly cave in –
This catastrophic shortlived reform
Directs to our homes the birds of heaven.
They come on farfetched winds to keep us warm.

Bribing these with bounty, we would rather
Forget our hopes of thaw when spring will clean
The boughs, dust from our sills snow and feather,
Release to its decay and true decline
The bittern whom this different weather
Cupboarded in ice like a specimen.

THE CENTAURS

The sergeant, an arrow in his back,
Who crawled, bleeding, up the dusty street,
Who gasped his news of the failed attack,
How on all fours he made his retreat –

He put the idea into our heads.
With such horrors fixed in the mind's eye,
Saying our prayers, fingering our beads
Half awake and half asleep we lie.

Since their secret weapon is the horse
Ten thousand hooves thunder in our ears.
A nightmare! and it is getting worse –
Our hopes on foot, galloping our fears.

Hands full of reins and spurs at their feet
They herd to an awkward river bend
Our squadrons who, certain of defeat,
Are wishing they had never listened.

Into the water our youth is spilled.
We make on the causeways our last stands.
Because of the bridge we did not build
Our whole army fights for balance.

Overcome however hard we fight,
Before us all the horsemen frowning
And, no opportunities for flight,
On either side a drop to drowning.

Is our way of life pedestrian?
Can these be the customs we defend
Slow aeon after slower aeon?
But, just as we think THIS IS THE END,

We wake to a world of infantry men.
We wake from nightmare into reason –
Of their reins and bridles not a sign.
We see another sun has risen,

And, our nightmare now a mystery tour,
At ease along the river's edges
Each cavalry man become a centaur,
The causeways growing into bridges.

PERSEPHONE

I

I see as through a skylight in my brain
The mole strew its buildings in the rain,

The swallows turn above their broken home
And all my acres in delirium.

II

Straitjacketed by cold and numskulled
Now sleep the welladjusted and the skilled –

The bat folds its wing like a winter leaf,
The squirrel in its hollow holds aloof.

III

The weasel and ferret, the stoat and fox
Move hand in glove across the equinox.

I can tell how softly their footsteps go –
Their footsteps borrow silence from the snow.

THE HEBRIDES

for Eavan Boland

I

The winds' enclosure, Atlantic's premises,
Last balconies
Above the waves, The Hebrides –
Too long did I postpone
Presbyterian granite and the lack of trees,
This orphaned stone

Day in, day out colliding with the sea.
Weather forecast,
Compass nor ordnance survey
Arranges my welcome
For, on my own, I have lost my way at last,
So far from home.

In whom the city is continuing,
I stop to look,
To find my feet among the ling
And bracken – over me
The bright continuum of gulls, a rook
Occasionally.

II

My eyes, slowly accepting panorama,
Try to include
In my original idea
The total effect
Of air and ocean – waterlogged all wood –
All harbours wrecked –

My dead-lights latched by whelk and barnacle
                    Till I abide
By the sea wall of the time I kill −
            My each nostalgic scheme
Jettisoned, as crises are, the further side
                    Of sleep and dream.

Between wind and wave this holiday
                    The cormorant,
    The oyster-catcher and osprey
            Proceed and keep in line
While I, hands in my pockets, hesitant,
                    Am in two minds.

III

Old neighbours, though shipwreck's my decision,
                    People my brain −
    Like breakwaters against the sun,
            Command in silhouette
My island circumstance − my cells retain,
                    Perpetuate

Their crumpled deportment through bad weather.
                    And I feel them
        Put on their raincoats for ever
            And walk out in the sea.
I am, though each one waves a phantom limb,
                    The amputee,

For these are my sailors, these my drowned −
                    In their heart of hearts,
        In their city I ran aground.
                Along my arteries
Sluice those homewaters petroleum hurts.
                    Dry dock, gantries,

Dykes of apparatus educate my bones
              To track the buoys
      Up sea lanes love emblazons
              To streets where shall conclude
My journey back from flux to poise, from poise
              To attitude.

Here, at the edge of my experience,
              Another tide
      Along the broken shore extends
              A lifetime's wrack and ruin –
No flotsam I may beachcomb now can hide
              That water line.

                    IV
Beyond the lobster pots where plankton spreads
              Porpoises turn.
      Seals slip over the cockle beds.
              Undertow dishevels
Seaweed in the shallows – and I discern
              My sea levels.

To right and left of me there intervene
              The tumbled burns –
      And these, on turf and boulder weaned,
              Confuse my calendar –
Their tilt is suicidal, their great return
              Curricular.

No matter what repose holds shore and sky
              In harmony,
      From this place in the long run I,
              Though here I might have been
Content with rivers where they meet the sea,
              Remove upstream,

Where the salmon, risking fastest waters –
Waterfall and rock
And the effervescent otters –
On bridal pools insist
As with fin and generation they unlock
The mountain's fist.

V

Now, buttoned up, with water in my shoes,
Clouds around me,
I can, through mist that misconstrues,
Read like a palimpsest
My past – those landmarks and that scenery
I dare resist.

Into my mind's unsympathetic trough
They fade away –
And to alter my perspective
I feel in the sharp cold
Of my vantage point too high above the bay
The sea grow old.

Granting the trawlers far below their stance,
Their anchorage,
I fight all the way for balance –
In the mountain's shadow
Losing foothold, covet the privilege
Of vertigo.

A WORKING HOLIDAY

for Colin Middleton

Water through the window, the light and shade
Fill up my head once more as I distil
All that sunshine in the glass of lemonade
John left overnight on the windowsill.

And though it was the far end of my teens
I can hear him ringing bells, hear his shout –
Though my Greek's now locked in the past tense
Down the long corridors I just make out

Our classics master – 'very eccentric' –
Breaking the dreams of our three weeks' stay
To get us up for breakfast and for Greek
'Because this is a working holiday.'

Into the back of my mind it all fits –
The house by the lake, Mrs Quirk
– The Keeper of the Two Colossal Tits –
Who came in to cook and do the housework.

The scholarly boy we all misunderstood,
His voice breaking, ahead of us a year,
Buck teeth champing the subjunctive mood.
His nickname was LAGOS – the Greek for HARE.

David swam naked in the pouring rain,
His foreskin like a turkey's wattle.
John's glass eye a shard of porcelain –
My comrades in the morning doing battle

With the Greek New Testament again – Acts
Of the Apostles – each of us a warden
Of views beyond our books which now contract
To Mrs Quirk by lunchtime in the garden

Gliding towards us like a huge balloon,
Behind her the water where the boat was –
The old boat which, even that afternoon,
Would be too frail to stomach all of us.

A HEADSTONE

Inscribed 'This stone claims five graves'

It told us, through the histories it lacked,
That always it grows harder to make clear
We loved, however carefully is stacked
The precious lumber that we shoulder here,
However biographical the gear:
That lives and where they end can so contract.

The sad allotment and the words we read
Owned not one date or title to undo
The silence of those people in their bed:
But someone kept like us this rendezvous –
The sinking he had launched their coffins into
Prolonged by love, till death mislaid his dead.

WORDS FOR JAZZ PERHAPS

for Solly Lipsitz

Elegy for Fats Waller

Lighting up, lest all our hearts should break,
His fiftieth cigarette of the day,
Happy with so many notes at his beck
And call, he sits there taking it away,
The maker of immaculate slapstick.

With music and with such precise rampage
Across the deserts of the blues a trail
He blazes, towards the one true mirage,
Enormous on a nimble-footed camel
And almost refusing to be his age.

He plays for hours on end and though there be
Oases one part water, two parts gin,
He tumbles past to reign, wise and thirsty,
At the still centre of his loud dominion –
THE SHOOK THE SHAKE THE SHEIKH OF ARABY.

Bud Freeman in Belfast

Fog horn and factory siren intercept
Each fragile hoarded-up refrain. What else
Is there to do but let those notes erupt

Until your fading last glissando settles
Among all other sounds – carefully wrapped
In the cotton wool from aspirin bottles?

To Bessie Smith

You bring from Chattanooga Tennessee
Your huge voice to the back of my mind
Where, like sea shells salvaged from the sea
As bright reminders of a few weeks' stay,
Some random notes are all I ever find.
I couldn't play your records every day.

I think of Tra-na-rossan, Inisheer,
Of Harris drenched by horizontal rain –
Those landscapes I must visit year by year.
I do not live with sounds so seasonal
Nor set up house for good. Your blues contain
Each longed-for holiday, each terminal.

To Bix Beiderbecke

In hotel rooms, in digs you went to school.
These dead were voices from the floor below
Who filled like an empty room your skull,

Who shared your perpetual one-night stand
– The havoc there, and the manoeuvrings! –
Each coloured hero with his instrument.

You were bound with one original theme
To compose in your head your terminus,
Or to improvise with the best of them

That parabola from blues to barrelhouse.

IN MEMORIAM

My father, let no similes eclipse
Where crosses like some forest simplified
Sink roots into my mind; the slow sands
Of your history delay till through your eyes
I read you like a book. Before you died,
Re-enlisting with all the broken soldiers
You bent beneath your rucksack, near collapse,
In anecdote rehearsed and summarised
These words I write in memory. Let yours
And other heartbreaks play into my hands.

Now I see in close-up, in my mind's eye,
The cracked and splintered dead for pity's sake
Each dismal evening predecease the sun,
You, looking death and nightmare in the face
With your kilt, harmonica and gun,
Grow older in a flash, but none the wiser
(Who, following the wrong queue at The Palace,
Have joined the London Scottish by mistake),
Your nineteen years uncertain if and why
Belgium put the kibosh on the Kaiser.

Between the corpses and the soup canteens
You swooned away, watching your future spill.
But, as it was, your proper funeral urn
Had mercifully smashed to smithereens,
To shrapnel shards that sliced your testicle.
That instant I, your most unlikely son,
In No Man's Land was surely left for dead,
Blotted out from your far horizon.
As your voice now is locked inside my head,
I yet was held secure, waiting my turn.

Finally, that lousy war was over.
Stranded in France and in need of proof
You hunted down experimental lovers,
Persuading chorus girls and countesses:
This, father, the last confidence you spoke.
In my twentieth year your old wounds woke
As cancer. Lodging under the same roof
Death was a visitor who hung about,
Strewing the house with pills and bandages,
Till he chose to put your spirit out.

Though they overslept the sequence of events
Which ended with the ambulance outside,
You lingering in the hall, your bowels on fire,
Tears in your eyes, and all your medals spent,
I summon girls who packed at last and went
Underground with you. Their souls again on hire,
Now those lost wives as recreated brides
Take shape before me, materialise.
On the verge of light and happy legend
They lift their skirts like blinds across your eyes.

AFTERMATH

Imagine among these meadows
Where the soldiers sink to dust
An aftermath with swallows
Lifting blood on their breasts
Up to the homely gables, and like
A dark cross overhead the hawk.

CHRISTOPHER AT BIRTH

Your uncle, totem and curator bends
Above your cot. It is you I want to see.
Your cry comes out like an eleison.
Only the name tag round your wrist extends
My surprised compassion to loyalty.
Your mother tells me you are my godson.

The previous room still moulds your shape
Which lies unwashed, out of its element,
Smelling like rain on soil. I stoop to lift
You out of bed and into my landscape,
Last arrival, obvious immigrant
Wearing the fashions of the place you left.

As winds are balanced in a swaying tree
I cradle your cries. And in my arms reside,
Till you fall asleep, your uncontended
Demands that the world be your nursery.
And I, a spokesman of that world outside,
Creation's sponsor, stand dumbfounded,

Although there is such a story to unfold
– Whether as forecast or reminder –
Of cattle steaming in their byres, and sheep
Beneath a hedge, arranged against the cold,
Our cat at home blinking by the fender,
The wolf treading its circuits towards sleep.

THE FREEMARTIN

Comes into her own
(Her barren increments,
Her false dawn)

As excess baggage,
A currency defaced –
Quaint coinage

To farmhands, farmers
Crossing the yard
With lamps in the small hours

For such incorrigibles,
Difficult births
In byres and stables.

GATHERING MUSHROOMS

Exhaled at dawn with the cattle's breath
Out of the reticent illfitting earth,

Acre on acre the mushrooms grew –
Bonus and bounty socketed askew.

Across the fields, as though to confound
Our processions and those underground

Accumulations, secret marriages,
We drew together by easy stages.

IN A CONVENT CEMETERY

Although they've been gone for ages
On their morning walk just beyond
The icons and the cabbages,
Convening out of sight and sound
To turn slowly their missal pages,

They find us here of all places,
And I abandon to the weather
And these unlikely mistresses
Where they bed down together,
Your maidenhair, your nightdresses.

MAN FRIDAY

So much is implied on that furthest strand –
The stranger's face of course, his outstretched hand,

Houses and harbours, shillings, pence and wars,
Troy's seven layers, the canals of Mars.

To lighthouse-keepers and their like I say –
Let solitude be named Man Friday:

Our folk may muster then, even the dead,
Footprint follow footprint through my head.

LEAVING INISHMORE

Rain and sunlight and the boat between them
Shifted whole hillsides through the afternoon –
Quiet variations on an urgent theme
Reminding me now that we left too soon
The island awash in wave and anthem.

Miles from the brimming enclave of the bay
I hear again the Atlantic's voices,
The gulls above us as we pulled away –
So munificent their final noises
These are the broadcasts from our holiday.

Oh, the crooked walkers on that tilting floor!
And the girls singing on the upper deck
Whose hair took the light like a downpour –
Interim nor change of scene shall shipwreck
Those folk on the move between shore and shore.

Summer and solstice as the seasons turn
Anchor our boat in a perfect standstill,
The harbour wall of Inishmore astern
Where the Atlantic waters overspill –
I shall name this the point of no return

Lest that excursion out of light and heat
Take on a January idiom –
Our ocean icebound when the year is hurt,
Wintertime past cure – the curriculum
Vitae of sailors and the sick at heart.

HOMAGE TO DR JOHNSON

for Philip Hobsbaum

I

The Hebridean gales mere sycophants,
So many loyal Boswells at his heel –
Yet the farflung outposts of experience
In the end undo a Roman wall,

The measured style. London is so far;
Each windswept strait he would encompass
Gives the unsinkable lexicographer
His reflection in its shattered glass.

He trudges off in the mist and the rain
Where only the thickest skin survives,
Among the rocks construes himself again,
Lifts through those altering perspectives

His downcast eyes, riding out the brainstorm,
His weatherproof enormous head at home.

II

There was no place to go but his own head
Where hard luck lodged as in an orphanage
With the desperate and the underfed.

So, surgeon himself to his dimensions,
The words still unembarrassed by their size,
He corrected death in its declensions,

The waters breaking where he stabbed the knife,
Washing his pockmarked body like a reef.

JOURNEY OUT OF ESSEX

or, John Clare's Escape from the Madhouse

I am lying with my head
Over the edge of the world,
Unpicking my whereabouts
Like the asylum's name
That they stitch on the sheets.

Sick now with bad weather
Or a virus from the fens,
I dissolve in a puddle
My biographies of birds
And the names of flowers.

That they may recuperate
Alongside the stunned mouse,
The hedgehog rolled in leaves,
I am putting to bed
In this rheumatic ditch

The boughs of my harvest-home,
My wives, one on either side,
And keeping my head low as
A lark's nest, my feet toward
Helpston and the pole star.

RIP VAN WINKLE

You wake to find all history collapsed,
The moon in purdah and the sun eclipsed.

Turn back the newsreel of the time you killed
To the dear departed, Rip Van Winkle.

Project for us the faces of the dead,
Unlock the Sleepy Hollow of your head.

BIRTHMARKS
for D.M.

You alone read every birthmark,
Only for you the tale it tells –
Idiot children in the dark
Whom we shall never bring to light,
Criminals in their prison cells –
These are the poems we cannot write.

Though we deny them name and birth,
Locked out from rhyme and lexicon
The ghosts still gather round our hearth
Whose bed and board makes up the whole –
Thief, murderer and clown – icon
And lares of the poet's soul.

II

AN EXPLODED VIEW
(1973)

for Derek, Seamus & Jimmy

We are trying to make ourselves heard
Like the lover who mouths obscenities
In his passion, like the condemned man
Who makes a last-minute confession,
Like the child who cries out in the dark.

TO THE POETS

The dying fall, the death spasm,
Last words and catechism –

These are the ways we spend our breath,
The epitaphs we lie beneath –

Silent departures going with
The nose flute and the penis sheath.

LARES

for Raymond Warren

Farls

Cut with a cross, they are propped
Before the fire: it will take
Mug after mug of stewed tea,
Inches of butter to ease
Christ's sojourn in a broken
Oatmeal farl down your throat.

Bridget

Her rush cross over the door
Brings Bridget the cowherd home,
Milk to the dandelion,
Bread to the doorstep, the sun's
Reflection under her foot
Like a stone skimmed on water.

Furrows

My arm supporting your spine
I lay you out beneath me
Until it is your knuckles,
The small bones of foot and hand
Strewing a field where the plough
Swerves and my horses stumble.

Beds

The livestock in the yard first,
Then the cattle in the field
But especially the bees
Shall watch our eyelids lower,
Petal and sod folding back
To make our beds lazy-beds.

Neighbours

Your hand in mine as you sleep
Makes my hand a bad neighbour
Who is moving through stable
And byre, or beside the well
Stooping to skim from your milk
The cream, the dew from your fields.

Patrick

As though it were Christ's ankle
He stoops to soothe in his hand
The stone's underside: whose spine's
That ridge of first potatoes,
Whose face the duckweed spreading
On a perfect reflection.

A NATIVITY

Dog

He will be welcome to
His place in the manger,
Anaesthetist and surgeon
Muffling the child's cries
And biting through the cord
That joins God to Mary.

She-goat

A protective midwife
She roots out with her horns
A sour cake from the straw
And, jaws grinding sideways,
Devours the afterbirth
Of the child of heaven.

Bullocks

They will make a present
Of their empty purses,
Their perfected music
An interval between
The man with the scissors
And the man with the knife.

Bullfinch

Slipped in by an old master
At the edge of the picture,
An idea in Mary's head,
A splash of colour –
Thistle-tweaker, theologian,
Eater-of-thorns.

CARAVAN

A rickety chimney suggests
The diminutive stove,
Children perhaps, the pots
And pans adding up to love –

So much concentrated under
The low roof, the windows
Shuttered against snow and wind,
That you would be magnified

(If you were there) by the dark,
Wearing it like an apron
And revolving in your hands
As weather in a glass dome,

The blizzard, the day beyond
And – tiny, barely in focus –
Me disappearing out of view
On probably the only horse,

Cantering off to the right
To collect the week's groceries,
Or to be gone for good
Having drawn across my eyes

Like a curtain all that light
And the snow, my history
Stiffening with the tea towels
Hung outside the door to dry.

THE ROPE-MAKERS

Sometimes you and I are like rope-makers
Twisting straw into a golden cable,
So gradual my walking backwards
You fail to notice when I reach the door,
Each step infinitesimal, a delay,
Neither a coming nor a going when
Across the lane-way I face you still
Or, at large at last in the sunny fields,
Struggle to pick you out of the darkness
Where, close to the dresser, the scrubbed table,
Fingers securing the other end, you
Watch me diminish in a square of light.

LOVE POEM

I

You define with your perfume
Infinitely shifting zones
And print in falls of talcum
The shadow of your foot.

II

Gossamers spin from your teeth,
So many light constructions
Describing as with wet wings
The gully under my tongue.

III

These wide migrations begin
In our seamier districts –
A slumdweller's pigeons
Released from creaking baskets.

THE ADULTERER

I have laid my adulteries
Beneath the floorboards, then resettled
The linoleum so that
The pattern aligns exactly,

Or, when I bundled into the cupboard
Their loose limbs, their heads,
I papered over the door
And cut a hole for the handle.

There they sleep with their names,
My other women, their underwear
Disarranged a little,
Their wounds closing slowly.

I have watched in the same cracked cup
Each separate face dissolve,
Their dispositions
Cluster like tea leaves,

Folding a silence about my hands
Which infects the mangle,
The hearth rug, the kitchen chair
I've been meaning to get mended.

SWANS MATING

Even now I wish that you had been there
Sitting beside me on the riverbank:
The cob and his pen sailing in rhythm
Until their small heads met and the final
Heraldic moment dissolved in ripples.

This was a marriage and a baptism,
A holding of breath, nearly a drowning,
Wings spread wide for balance where he trod,
Her feathers full of water and her neck
Under the water like a bar of light.

GALAPAGOS

Now you have scattered into islands –
Breasts, belly, knees, the mount of Venus,
Each a Galapagos of the mind
Where you, the perfect stranger, prompter
Of throw-backs, of hold-ups in time,

Embody peculiar animals –
The giant tortoise hesitating,
The shy lemur, the iguana's
Slow gaze in which the *Beagle* anchors
With its homesick scientist on board.

BADGER

for Raymond Piper

I

Pushing the wedge of his body
Between cromlech and stone circle,
He excavates down mine shafts
And back into the depths of the hill.

His path straight and narrow
And not like the fox's zig-zags,
The arc of the hare who leaves
A silhouette on the sky line.

Night's silence around his shoulders,
His face lit by the moon, he
Manages the earth with his paws,
Returns underground to die.

II

An intestine taking in
patches of dog's-mercury,
brambles, the bluebell wood;
a heel revolving acorns;
a head with a price on it
brushing cuckoo-spit, goose-grass;
a name that parishes borrow.

III

For the digger, the earth-dog
It is a difficult delivery
Once the tongs take hold,

Vulnerable his pig's snout
That lifted cow-pats for beetles,
Hedgehogs for the soft meat,

His limbs dragging after them
So many stones turned over,
The trees they tilted.

THE CORNER OF THE EYE

kingfisher

a knife-thrower
hurling himself, a rainbow
fractured against
the plate glass of winter:

his eye a water bead,
lens and meniscus where
the dragonfly drowns,
the water-boatman crawls.

wren

two wings criss-crossing
through gaps and loop-holes,
a mote melting towards
the corner of the eye:

or poised in the thicket
between adulteries,
small spaces circumscribed
by the tilt of his tail.

dipper

the cataract's deluge
and nightmare a curtain
he can go behind,
heavy water rolling

over feather and eye
its adhesive drops,
beneath his feet the spray
thickening into moss.

robin

breast a warning, he
shadows the heavy-
footed earth-breakers,
bull's hoof, pheasant's toe:

is an eye that would —
if we let it in — scan
the walls for cockroaches,
for bed-bugs the beds.

CASUALTY

Its decline was gradual,
A sequence of explorations
By other animals, each
Looking for the easiest way in –

A surgical removal of the eyes,
A probing of the orifices,
Bitings down through the skin,
Through tracts where the grasses melt,

And the bad air released
In a ceremonious wounding
So slow that more and more
I wanted to get closer to it.

A candid grin, the bones
Accumulating to a diagram
Except for the polished horns,
The immaculate hooves.

And this no final reduction
For the ribs began to scatter,
The wool to move outward
As though hunger still worked there,

As though something that had followed
Fox and crow was desperate for
A last morsel and was
Other than the wind or rain.

READINGS
for Peter Longley

I
I remember your eyes in bandages
And me reading to you like a mother;
Our grubby redeemer, the chimney-sweep
Whose baptism among the seaweed
Began when he stopped astounded beside
The expensive bed, the white coverlet,
The most beautiful girl he had ever seen –
Her hair on the eiderdown like algae,
Her face a reflection in clean water;
The Irishwoman haunting Tom's shoulder –
The shawl's canopy, the red petticoats
Arriving beside him again and again,
The white feet accompanying his feet,
All of the leafy roads down to the sea.

II
Other faces at the frosty window,
Kay and Gerda in their separate attics;
The icicle driven into Kay's heart –
Then a glance at the pillow where you
Twisted your head again and tried to squeeze
Light like a tear through the bandages.

LETTERS

returning over the nightmare ground
we found the place again . . .
                    Keith Douglas

To Three Irish Poets

I

This, the twentieth day of March
In the first year of my middle age,
Sees me the father of a son:
Now let him in your minds sleep on
Lopsided, underprivileged
And, out of his tight burrow edged,

Your godchild while you think of him
Or, if you can't accept the term,
Don't count the damage but instead
Wet, on me, the baby's head:
About his ears our province reels
Pulsating like his fontanel,

And I, with you, when I baptise
Must calculate, must improvise
The holy water and the font,
Anything else that he may want,
And, 'priest of the muses', mock the
Malevolent *deus loci*.

53

II

Now that the distant islands rise
Out of the corners of my eyes
And the imagination fills
Bog-meadow and surrounding hills,
I find myself addressing you
As though I'd always wanted to:

In order to take you all in
I've had to get beneath your skin,
To colonise you like a land,
To study each distinctive hand
And, by squatter's rights, inhabit
The letters of its alphabet,

Although when I call him Daniel
(Mother and baby doing well),
Lost relations take their places,
Namesakes and receding faces:
Late travellers on the Underground
People my head like a ghost town.

III

Over the cobbles I recall
Cattle clattering to the North Wall
Till morning and the morning's rain
Rinsed out the zig-zags of the brain,
Conducting excrement and fear
Along that lethal thoroughfare:

Now every lost bedraggled field
Like a mythopoeic bog unfolds
Its gelignite and dumdums:
And should the whole idea become
A vegetable run to seed in
Even our suburban garden,

We understudy for the hare's
Disappearance around corners,
The approximate untold barks
Of the otters we call water-dogs –
A dim reflection of ourselves,
A muddy forepaw that dissolves.

IV

Blood on the kerbstones, and my mind
Dividing like a pavement,
Cracked by the weeds, by the green grass
That covers our necropolis,
The pity, terror . . . What comes next
Is a lacuna in the text,

Only blots of ink conceding
Death or blackout as a reading:
For this, his birthday, must confound
Baedekers of the nightmare ground –
And room for him beneath the hedge
With succour, school and heritage

Is made tonight when I append
Each of your names and name a friend:
For yours, then, and the child's sake
I who have heard the waters break
Claim this my country, though today
Timor mortis conturbat me.

To James Simmons

We were distracted by too many things . . .
the wine, the jokes, the music, fancy gowns.
We were no good as murderers, we were clowns.

– Who stated with the Irish queer
A preference for girls to beer –
Here's an attempt at telling all,
My confession unilateral:
Not that it matters for my part
Because I have your lines by heart,

Because the poetry you write
Is the flicker of a night-light
Picking out where it is able
Objects on the dressing table,
Glancing through the great indoors
Where love and death debate the chores,

And where, beneath a breast, you see
The blue veins in filigree,
The dust in a glass of water,
In a discarded french letter
The millions acting out their last
Collaborations with the past.

Yes, to entertain your buddies
With such transcendental studies
Rather than harmonise with hams
In yards of penitential psalms
I count among your better turns:
Play your guitar while Derry burns,

Pipe us aboard the sinking ship
Two by two . . . But before the trip
A pause, please, while the hundredth line
Squanders itself in facile rhyme –
A spry exposé of our game
But paradigmatic all the same

Like talking on as the twelfth chime
Ends nineteen hundred and ninety-nine,
The millennium and number:
For never milestones, but the camber
Dictates this journey till we tire
(So much for perning in a gyre!):

True to no 'kindred points', astride
No iridescent arc besides,
Each gives the other's lines a twist
Over supper, dinner, breakfast
To make a sort of Moebius Band,
Eternal but quotidian . . .

So, post me some octosyllabics
As redolent of death and sex
Or keep this for the rainy days
When, mindful of the final phase,
We diagnose it a relapse,
A metric following the steps

Of an aging ballroom dancer
(Words a bow-tie round a cancer):
Or a reasonable way to move –
A Moonlight Saunter out to prove
That poetry, a tongue at play
With lip and tooth, is here to stay,

To exercise in metaphor
Our knockings at the basement door,
A ramrod mounted to invade
The vulva, Hades' palisade,
The Gates of Horn and Ivory
Or the Walls of Londonderry.

To Derek Mahon

And did we come into our own
When, minus muse and lexicon,
We traced in August sixty-nine
Our imaginary Peace Line
Around the burnt-out houses of
The Catholics we'd scarcely loved,
Two Sisyphuses come to budge
The sticks and stones of an old grudge,

Two poetic conservatives
In the city of guns and long knives,
Our ears receiving then and there
The stereophonic nightmare
Of the Shankill and the Falls,
Our matches struck on crumbling walls
To light us as we moved at last
Through the back alleys of Belfast?

Why it mattered to have you here
You who journeyed to Inisheer
With me, years back, one Easter when
With MacIntyre and the lone Dane

Our footsteps lifted up the larks
Echoing off those western rocks
And down that darkening arcade
Hung with the failures of our trade,

Will understand. We were tongue-tied
Companions of the island's dead
In the graveyard among the dunes,
Eavesdroppers on conversations
With a Jesus who spoke Irish –
We were strangers in that parish,
Black tea with bacon and cabbage
For our sacraments and pottage,

Dank blankets making up our Lent
Till, islanders ourselves, we bent
Our knees and cut the watery sod
From the lazy-bed where slept a God
We couldn't count among our friends,
Although we'd taken in our hands
Splinters of driftwood nailed and stuck
On the rim of the Atlantic.

That was Good Friday years ago –
How persistent the undertow
Slapped by currachs ferrying stones,
Moonlight glossing the confusions
Of its each bilingual wave – yes,
We would have lingered there for less . . .
Six islanders for a ten-bob note
Rowed us out to the anchored boat.

To Seamus Heaney

From Carrigskeewaun in Killadoon
I write, although I'll see you soon,
Hoping this fortnight detonates
Your year in the United States,
Offering you by way of welcome
To the sick counties we call home
The mystical point at which I tire
Of Calor gas and a turf fire.

Till we talk again in Belfast
Pleasanter far to leave the past
Across three acres and two brooks
On holiday in a post box
Which dripping fuchsia bells surround,
Its back to the prevailing wind,
And where sanderlings from Iceland
Court the breakers, take my stand,

Disinfecting with a purer air
That small subconscious cottage where
The Irish poet slams his door
On slow-worm, toad and adder:
Beneath these racing skies it is
A tempting stance indeed – *ipsis*
Hibernicis hiberniores –
Except that we know the old stories,

The midden of cracked hurley sticks
Tied to recall the crucifix,
Of broken bones and lost scruples,
The blackened hearth, the blazing gable's
Telltale cinder where we may
Scorch our shins until that day
We sleepwalk through a No Man's Land
Lipreading to an Orange band.

Continually, therefore, we rehearse
Goodbyes to all our characters
And, since both would have it both ways,
On the oily roll of calmer seas
Launch coffin-ship and life-boat,
Body with soul thus kept afloat,
Mind open like a half-door
To the speckled hill, the plovers' shore.

So let it be the lapwing's cry
That lodges in the throat as I
Raise its alarum from the mud,
Seeking for your sake to conclude
Ulster Poet our Union Title
And prolong this sad recital
By leaving careful footprints round
A wind-encircled burial mound.

KINDERTOTENLIEDER

There can be no songs for dead children
Near the crazy circle of explosions,
The splintering tangent of the ricochet,

No songs for the children who have become
My unrestricted tenants, fingerprints
Everywhere, teethmarks on this and that.

WOUNDS

Here are two pictures from my father's head —
I have kept them like secrets until now:
First, the Ulster Division at the Somme
Going over the top with 'Fuck the Pope!'
'No Surrender!': a boy about to die,
Screaming 'Give 'em one for the Shankill!'
'Wilder than Gurkhas' were my father's words
Of admiration and bewilderment.
Next comes the London-Scottish padre
Resettling kilts with his swagger-stick,
With a stylish backhand and a prayer.
Over a landscape of dead buttocks
My father followed him for fifty years.
At last, a belated casualty,
He said — lead traces flaring till they hurt —
'I am dying for King and Country, slowly.'
I touched his hand, his thin head I touched.

Now, with military honours of a kind,
With his badges, his medals like rainbows,
His spinning compass, I bury beside him
Three teenage soldiers, bellies full of
Bullets and Irish beer, their flies undone.
A packet of Woodbines I throw in,
A lucifer, the Sacred Heart of Jesus
Paralysed as heavy guns put out
The night-light in a nursery for ever;
Also a bus-conductor's uniform —
He collapsed beside his carpet-slippers
Without a murmur, shot through the head
By a shivering boy who wandered in
Before they could turn the television down
Or tidy away the supper dishes.
To the children, to a bewildered wife,
I think 'Sorry Missus' was what he said.

NIGHTMARE

In this dream I am carrying a pig,
Cradling in my arms its deceptive grin,
The comfortable folds of its baby limbs,
The feet coyly disposed like a spaniel's.

I am in charge of its delivery,
Taking it somewhere, and feeling oddly
And indissolubly attached to it –
There is nothing I can do about it,

Not even when it bites into my skull
Quite painlessly, and eats my face away,
Its juices corroding my memory,
The chamber of straight lines and purposes,

Until I am carrying everywhere
Always, on a dwindling zig-zag, the pig.

THE FAIRGROUND

There, in her stall between the tattooist
And the fortune-teller, all day she sits –
The fat lady who through a megaphone
Proclaims her measurements and poundage.
Contortionists, sword-swallowers, fire-eaters

As well as a man with no arms or legs
Who rolls his own cigarettes, managing
Tobacco-pouch, paper, the box of matches
With his mouth: painstaking the performance.
He wears his woollens like a sausage-skin.

Hidden behind the broken-down equipment
Are big foreheads, bow legs, stubby fingers –
Midgets in clowns' make-up and bowler hats:
And in flowered smocks, continuously dancing,
Cretins: a carousel of tiny skulls.

Then a theatrical change in the weather
So that I am the solitary spectator:
A drenched fairground, the company advancing
And it is my head they hold in their hands.
The eyes open and close like a doll's eyes.

POTEEN

Enough running water
To cool the copper worm,
The veins at the wrist,
Vitriol to scorch the throat –

And the brimming hogshead,
Reduced by one noggin-full
Sprinkled on the ground,
Becomes an affair of

Remembered souterrains,
Sunk workshops, out-backs,
The back of the mind –
The whole bog an outhouse

Where, alongside cudgels,
Guns, the informer's ear
We have buried it –
Blood-money, treasure-trove.

CONFESSIONS OF AN IRISH
ETHER-DRINKER

I

It freezes the puddles,
Films the tongue, its brief lozenge
Lesions of spittle and bile,
Dispersals of weather –

Icicles, bones in the ditch,
The blue sky splintering,
Water's fontanel
Closed like an eyelid.

II

My dialect becomes
Compactings of sea sounds,
The quietest drifts,
Each snowed-under
Cul-de-sac of the brain –
Glaucoma, pins and needles,
Fur on the tongue:

Or the hidden scythe
Probing farther than pain,
Its light buried in my ear,
The seed potatoes
Filling with blood –
Nuggets of darkness,
Silence's ovaries.

Impasto or washes as a rule:
Tuberous clottings, a muddy
Accumulation, internal rhyme –
Fuchsia's droop towards the ground,
The potato and its flower:

Or a continuing drizzle,
Specialisations of light,
Bog-water stretched over sand
In small waves, elisions –
The dialects of silence:

Or, sometimes, in combination
Outlining the bent spines,
The angular limbs of creatures –
Lost minerals colouring
The initial letter, the stance.

THE ISLAND

The one saddle and bit on the island
We set aside for every second Sunday
When the priest rides slowly up from the pier.
Afterwards his boat creaks into the mist.
Or he arrives here nine times out of ten
With the doctor. They will soon be friends.

Visitors are few. A Belgian for instance
Who has told us all about the oven,
Linguists occasionally, and sociologists.
A lapsed Capuchin monk who came to stay
Was first and last to fish the lake for eels.
His carved crucifixes are still on sale.

One ship continues to rust on the rocks.
We stripped it completely of wash-hand basins,
Toilet fitments, its cargo of linoleum
And have set up house in our own fashion.
We can estimate time by the shadow
Of a doorpost inching across the floor.

In the thatch blackbirds rummaging for worms
And our dead submerged beneath the dunes.
We count ourselves historians of sorts
And chronicle all such comings and goings.
We can walk in a day around the island.
We shall reach the horizon and disappear.

CARRIGSKEEWAUN

for Penny & David Cabot

The Mountain

This is ravens' territory, skulls, bones,
The marrow of these boulders supervised
From the upper air: I stand alone here
And seem to gather children about me,
A collection of picnic things, my voice
Filling the district as I call their names.

The Path

With my first step I dislodge the mallards
Whose necks strain over the bog to where
Kittiwakes scrape the waves: then, the circle
Widening, lapwings, curlews, snipe until
I am left with only one swan to nudge
To the far side of its gradual disdain.

The Strand

I discover, remaindered from yesterday,
Cattle tracks, a sanderling's tiny trail,
The footprints of the children and my own
Linking the dunes to the water's edge,
Reducing to sand the dry shells, the toe-
And fingernail parings of the sea.

The Wall

I join all the men who have squatted here
This lichened side of the drystone wall
And notice how smoke from our turf fire
Recalls in the cool air above the lake
Steam from a kettle, a tablecloth and
A table she might have already set.

The Lake

Though it will duplicate at any time
The sheep and cattle that wander there,
For a few minutes every evening
Its surface seems tilted to receive
The sun perfectly, the mare and her foal,
The heron, all such special visitors.

THE WEST

Beneath a gas-mantle that the moths bombard,
Light that powders at a touch, dusty wings,
I listen for news through the atmospherics,
A crackle of sea-wrack, spinning driftwood,
Waves like distant traffic, news from home,

Or watch myself, as through a sandy lens,
Materialising out of the heat-shimmers
And finding my way for ever along
The path to this cottage, its windows,
Walls, sun and moon dials, home from home.

IN MEMORY OF GERARD DILLON

I

You walked, all of a sudden, through
The rickety gate which opens
To a scatter of curlews,
An acre of watery light; your grave
A dip in the dunes where sand mislays
The sound of the sea, earth over you
Like a low Irish sky; the sun
An electric light bulb clouded
By the sandy tides, sunlight lost
And found, a message in a bottle.

II

You are a room full of self-portraits,
A face that follows us everywhere;
An ear to the ground listening for
Dead brothers in layers; an eye
Taking in the beautiful predators –
Cats on the windowsill, birds of prey
And, between the diminutive fields,
A dragonfly, wings full of light
Where the road narrows to the last farm.

III

Christening robes, communion dresses,
The shawls of factory workers,
A blind drawn on the Lower Falls.

SKARA BRAE

for Sheila & Denis Smyth

A window into the ground,
The bumpy lawn in section,
An exploded view
Through middens, through lives,

The thatch of grass roots,
The gravelly roof compounding
Periwinkles, small bones,
A calendar of meals,

The thread between sepulchre
And home a broken necklace,
Knuckles, dice scattering
At the warren's core,

Pebbles the tide washes
That conceded for so long
Living room, the hard beds,
The table made of stone.

GHOST TOWN

I have located it, my ghost town –
A place of interminable afternoons,
Sad cottages, scythes rusting in the thatch;
Of so many hesitant surrenders to
Enfolding bog, the scuts of bog cotton.

The few residents include one hermit
Persisting with a goat and two kettles
Among the bracken, a nervous spinster
In charge of the post office, a lighthouse-keeper
Who emerges to collect his groceries.

Since no one has got around to it yet
I shall restore the sign which reads CINEMA,
Rescue from the verge of invisibility
The faded stills of the last silent feature –
I shall become the local eccentric:

Already I have retired there to fill
Several gaps in my education –
The weather's ways, a handful of neglected
Pentatonic melodies and, after a while,
Dialect words for the parts of the body.

Indeed, with so much on my hands, family
And friends are definitely not welcome –
Although by the time I am accepted there
(A reputation and my own half-acre)
I shall have written another letter home.

THREE POSTHUMOUS PIECES

I

In lieu of my famous last words or
The doctor's hushed diagnosis
Lifting like a draught from the door
My oracular pages, this
Will have fluttered on to the floor –
The first of my posthumous pieces.

II

As a sort of accompaniment
Drafted in different-coloured inks
Through several notebooks, this is meant
To read like a riddle from the Sphinx
And not my will and testament –
No matter what anybody thinks.

III

Two minuses become a plus
When, at the very close of play
And with the minimum of fuss,
I shall permit myself to say:
This is my Opus Posthumous –
An inspiration in its way.

ALTERA CITHERA

A change of tune, then,
On another zither,
A new aesthetic, or
The same old songs
That are out of key,
Unwashed by epic oceans
And dipped by love
In lyric waters only?

> Given under our hand
> (With a ballpoint pen)
> After the Latin of Gaius
> Sextus Propertius,
> An old friend, the shadow
> Of his former self
> Who – and this I append
> Without his permission –

Loaded the dice before
He put them in his sling
And aimed at history,
Bringing to the ground
Like lovers Caesar,
Soldiers, politicians
And all the dreary
Epics of the muscle-bound.

DOCTOR JAZZ

Hello, Central! Give me Doctor Jazz!

Jelly Roll Morton

To be nearly as great as you
Think you are, play the same tunes
Again and again: small fortunes,
Diamonds for each hollow tooth.

Django Reinhardt

A whole new method compensates
For your damaged fingers: sweat
In the creases of your forehead,
Mother-of-pearl between the frets.

King Oliver

Now all pretenders to the throne
Learn how the patient gums decay,
Music hurts: though they took away
Your bad breath, the crown's your own.

Billie Holiday

You fastened to your bony thigh
Some dollar bills and waited for
The cacophonous janitor
And silence and the cue to die.

ALIBIS

My botanical studies took me among
Those whom I now consider my ancestors.
I used to appear to them at odd moments –
With buckets of water in the distance, or
At the campfire, my arms full of snowy sticks.
Beech mast, hedgehogs, cresses were my diet,
My medicaments badger grease and dock leaves.
A hard life. Nevertheless, they named after me
A clover that flourished on those distant slopes.
Later I found myself playing saxophone
On the Souza Band's Grand Tour of the World.
Perhaps because so much was happening
I started, in desperation, to keep a diary.
(I have no idea what came over me.)
After that I sat near a sunny window
Waiting for pupils among the music-stands.
At present I am drafting appendices
To lost masterpieces, some of them my own –
Requiems, entertainments for popes and kings.
From time to time I choose to express myself
In this manner, the basic line. Indeed,
My one remaining ambition is to be
The last poet in Europe to find a rhyme.

II

I wanted this to be a lengthy meditation
With myself as the central character –
Official guide through the tall pavilions
Or even the saviour of damaged birds.
I accepted my responsibilities
And was managing daily after matins
And before lunch my stint of composition.
But gradually, as though I had planned it,
And with only a few more pages to go

Of my *Apologia Pro Vita Mea,*
There dawned on me this idea of myself
Clambering aboard an express train full of
Honeymoon couples and football supporters.
I had folded my life like a cheque book,
Wrapped my pyjamas around two noggins
To keep, for a while at least, my visions warm.
Tattered and footloose in my final phase
I improvised on the map of the world
And hurtled to join, among the police files,
My obstreperous bigfisted brothers.

III

I could always have kept myself to myself
And, falling asleep with the light still on,
Reached the quiet conclusion that this
(And this is where I came in) was no more than
The accommodation of different weathers,
Whirlwind tours around the scattered islands,
Telephone calls from the guilty suburbs,
From the back of the mind, a simple question
Of being in two places at the one time.

OPTIONS

for Michael Allen

Ha! here's three on 's are sophisticated.
Thou art the thing itself.

These were my options: firstly
To have gone on and on –
A garrulous correspondence
Between me, the ideal reader
And – a halo to high-light
My head – that outer circle
Of critical intelligences
Deciphering – though with telling
Lacunae – my life-story,
Holding up to the bright mirrors
Of expensive libraries
My candours in palimpsest,
My collected blotting papers.

Or, at a pinch, I could have
Implied in reduced haiku
A world of suffering, swaddled
In white silence like babies
The rows of words, the mono-
Syllabic titles – my brain sore
And, as I struggled to master
The colon, my poet's tongue
Scorched by nicotine and coffee,
By the voracious acids
Of my *Ars Poetica,*
My clenched fist – towards midnight –
A paperweight on the language.

Or a species of skinny stanza
Might have materialised
In laborious versions
After the Finnish, for epigraph
The wry juxtaposing of
Wise-cracks by Groucho or Mae West
And the hushed hexameters
Of the right pastoral poet
From the Silver Age – Bacchylides
For instance – the breathings reversed,
The accents wrong mostly – proof,
If such were needed, of my humour
Among the big dictionaries.

These were my options, I say –
Night-lights, will-o'-the-wisps
Out of bog-holes and dark corners
Pointing towards the asylum
Where, for a quid of tobacco
Or a snatch of melody,
I might have cut off my head
In so many words – to borrow
A diagnosis of John Clare's –
Siphoning through the ears
Letters of the alphabet
And, with the vowels and consonants,
My life of make-believe.

TUTANKHAMUN

That could be me lying there
Surrounded by furniture,
My interest vested in
The persistence of objects,
An affectionate household;
The surrender of the bolt,
The wheeze of dusty hinges
Almost pleasurable
After the prolonged slumber
At my permanent address;
Cerements and substance
A sensational disclosure –
My various faces
Upside down in the spoons.

AN IMAGE FROM PROPERTIUS

My head is melting,
Its cinder burnt for this:

Ankle-bone, knuckle
In the ship of death,

A load five fingers gather
Pondered by the earth.

III

MAN LYING ON A WALL
(1976)

for Becky, Dan & Sarah

No insulation –
A house full of draughts,
Visitors, friends:

Its warmth escaping –
The snow on our roof
The first to melt.

CHECK-UP

Let this be my check-up:
Head and ear on my chest
To number the heartbeats,
Fingertips or your eyes
Taking in the wrinkles
And folds, and your body

Weighing now my long bones,
In the palm of your hand
My testicles, future:
Because if they had to
The children would eat me –
There's no such place as home.

THE LODGER

The lodger is writing a novel.
We give him the run of the house
But he occupies my mind as well –
An attic, a lumber-room
For his typewriter, notebooks,
The slowly accumulating pages.

At the end of each four-fingered
Suffering line the angelus rings –
A hundred noons and sunsets
As we lie here whispering,
Careful not to curtail our lives
Or change the names he has given us.

THE SWIM

The little rowing boat was full of
Friends and their intelligent children,
One of them bailing out for dear life
It seemed, while with an indolent hand

Another trailed a V on the lake
And directed it towards the island
Like an arrow. And nobody looked
As we undressed quickly and jumped in.

All of you vanished except your head:
Shoulders dissolving, and your arms too,
So opaque the element which could,
I knew, bend a stick at the elbow

Or, taking the legs from under you,
In its cat's-cradle of cross-currents
Like a bridegroom lift you bodily
Over the threshold to the island.

To risk brambles and nettles because
We wanted to make love there and then
In spite of the mud between my toes,
The weeds showing like veins on your skin,

Did seem all that remained to be done
As the creak of the rowlocks faded
And our friends left us to be alone
Or whatever they had decided.

THE BAT

We returned to the empty ballroom
And found a bat demented there, quite
Out of its mind, flashing round and round
Where earlier the dancers had moved.

We opened a window and shouted
To jam the signals and, so we thought,
Inspire a tangent in the tired skull,
A swerve, a saving miscalculation.

We had come to make love secretly
Without disturbance or obstacle,
And fell like shadows across the bat's
Singlemindedness, sheer insanity.

I told you of the blind snake that thrives
In total darkness by eating bats,
Of centuries measured in bat droppings,
The light bones that fall out of the air.

You called it a sky-mouse and described
Long fingers, anaesthetising teeth,
How it clung to the night by its thumbs,
And suggested that we leave it there.

Suspended between floor and ceiling
It would continue in our absence
And drop exhausted, a full stop
At the centre of the ballroom floor.

THE GOOSE

Remember the white goose in my arms,
A present still. I plucked the long
Flight-feathers, down from the breast,
Finest fuzz from underneath the wings.

I thought of you through the operation
And covered the unmolested head,
The pink eyes that had persisted in
An expression of disappointment.

It was right to hesitate before
I punctured the skin, made incisions
And broached with my reluctant fingers
The chill of its intestines, because

Surviving there, lodged in its tract,
Nudging the bruise of the orifice
Was the last egg. I delivered it
Like clean bone, a seamless cranium.

Much else followed which, for your sake,
I bundled away, burned on the fire
With the head, the feet, the perfect wings.
The goose was ready for the oven.

I would boil the egg for your breakfast,
Conserve for weeks the delicate fats
As in the old days. In the meantime
We dismantled it, limb by limb.

LOVE POEM

If my nose could smell only
You and what you are about,
If my fingertips, tongue, mouth
Could trace your magnetic lines,
Your longitudes, latitudes,
If my eyes could see no more
Than dust accumulating
Under your hair, your skin's
Removals and departures,
The glacial progression
Of your fingernails, toenails,
If my ears could hear nothing
But the noise of your body's
Independent processes,
Lungs, heartbeat, intestines,
Then I would be lulled in sleep
That soothes for a lifetime
The scabby knees of boyhood,
And alters the slow descent
Of the scrotum towards death.

BELLADONNA

I

Mischievous berries release the drug
That whitens her complexion and makes
Black pools of the pupils of her eyes,
Her face reflecting my face, eyelids
A sparrow watering its wings there
Or a butterfly drowned in the cup.

II

I have surrounded her with bottles
– Whiskey, medicines, assorted drugs –
I am a drunk, an addict, and she
The genie behind the glass, released
When I drink at her mouth, when I smell
Through her nostrils these substances.

III

She and I are blood donors, prepared
As specimens for the microscope,
Transparencies of Christ's example
And, as anybody's future now,
Strangers, our identities smothered
Under the wing of the pelican.

DESERT WARFARE

Though there are distances between us
I lean across and with my finger
Pick sleep from the corners of her eyes,
Two grains of sand. Could any soldier
Conscripted to such desert warfare
Discern more accurately than I do
The numerous hazards – a high sun,
Repetitive dunes, compasses jamming,
Delirium, death – or dare with me
During the lulls in each bombardment
To address her presence, her absence?
She might be a mirage, and my long
Soliloquies part of the action.

IN MAYO

I

For her sake once again I disinter
Imagination like a brittle skull
From where the separating vertebrae
And scapulae litter a sandy wind,

As though to reach her I must circle
This burial mound, its shadow turning
Under the shadow of a seabird's wing:
A sundial for the unhallowed soul.

II

Though the townland's all ears, all eyes
To decipher our movements, she and I
Appear on the scene at the oddest times:
We follow the footprints of animals,

Then vanish into the old wives' tales
Leaving behind us landmarks to be named
After our episodes, and the mushrooms
That cluster where we happen to lie.

III

When it is time for her to fall asleep
And I touch her eyelids, may night itself,
By my rule of thumb, be no profounder
Than the grassy well among irises

Where wild duck shelter their candid eggs:
No more beguiling than a gull's feather
In whose manifold gradations of light
I clothe her now and erase the scene.

IV

Dawns and dusks here should consist of
Me scooping a hollow for her hip-bone,
The stony headland a bullaun, a cup
To balance her body in like water:

Then a slow awakening to the swans
That fly home in twos, married for life,
Larks nestling beside the cattle's feet
And snipe the weight of the human soul.

DREAMS

I

Your face with hair
Falling over it
Was all of your mind
That I understood,

At the bottom of which
Like a windfall
I lay and waited
For your eyes to open.

II

I am a hot head
That quits the pillow,
A pair of feet
Numb with nightmare

Near the chilly lake
Of faithful swans
Or the clean mating
Of wolves in the snow.

LANDSCAPE

Here my imagination
Tangles through a turfstack
Like skeins of sheep's wool:
Is a bull's horn silting
With powdery seashells.

I am clothed, unclothed
By racing cloud shadows,
Or else disintegrate
Like a hillside neighbour
Erased by sea mist.

A place of dispersals
Where the wind fractures
Flight-feathers, insect wings
And rips thought to tatters
Like a fuchsia petal.

For seconds, dawn or dusk,
The sun's at an angle
To read inscriptions by:
The splay of the badger
And the otter's skidmarks

Melting into water
Where a minnow flashes:
A mouth drawn to a mouth
Digests the glass between
Me and my reflection.

WEATHER

I carry indoors
Two circles of blue sky,
Splinters of sunlight
As spring water tilts
And my buckets, heavy

Under the pressure of
Enormous atmospheres,
Two lakes and the islands
Enlarging constantly,
Tug at my shoulders, or,

With a wet sky low as
The ceiling, I shelter
Landmarks, keep track of
Animals, all the birds
In a reduced outdoors

And open my windows,
The wings of dragonflies
Hung from an alder cone,
A raindrop enclosing
Brookweed's five petals.

FLORA

A flutter of leaves
And pages open
Where, as my bookmark,
A flower is pressed,

Calyx, filament,
Anther staining
These pictures of me
In waste places

Shadowing sheep-tracks
From seacliff to dunes,
Ditches that drain
The salty marshes,

Naming the outcasts
Where petal and bud
Colour a runnel
Or sodden pasture,

Where bell and bugle,
A starry cluster
Or butterfly wing
Convey me farther

And in memory
And hands deposit
Blue periwinkles,
Meadowsweet, tansy.

POINTS OF THE COMPASS

for John Hewitt

Inscription

A stone inscribed with a cross,
The four points of the compass
Or a confluence of lines,
Crossroads and roundabout:
Someone's last milestone, propped
At an angle to the nettles,
A station that staggers still
Through tendrils of silverweed:
To understand what it says
I have cleared this area
Next to the casual arc
A thorn traces upon stone.

Clapper Bridge

One way to proceed:
Taking the water step
By step, stepping stones
With a roof over them,
A bed of standing stones,
Watery windows sunk
Into a drystone wall,
Porches for the water,
Some twists completing it
And these imperfections
Set, like the weather,
On the eve of mending.

Cell

After the entire structure
Has been sited thoughtfully
To straddle a mountain stream,
The ideal plan would include
A path leading from woodland,
From sorrel and watercress
To the one door, a window
Framing the salmon weir,
A hole for smoke, crevices
For beetles or saxifrage
And, for the fear of flooding,
Room enough under the floor.

Standing Stone

Where two lakes suggest petals
Of vetch or the violet,
The wings of a butterfly,
Ink blots reflecting the mind,
There, to keep them apart
As versions of each other,
To record the distances
Between islands of sunlight
And, as hub of the breezes,
To administer the scene
From its own peninsula,
A stone stands, a standing stone.

FLEADH

for Brian O'Donnell

Fiddle

Stained with blood from a hare,
Then polished with beeswax
It suggests the vibration
Of diaphanous wings
Or – bow, elbow dancing –
Follows the melted spoors
Where fast heels have spun
Dewdrops in catherine-wheels.

Flute

Its ebony and silver
Mirror a living room
Where disembodied fingers
Betray to the darkness
Crevices, every knothole –
Hearth and chimney-corner
For breezes igniting
The last stick of winter.

Bodhran

We have eaten the goat:
Now his discarded horns
From some farflung midden
Call to his skin, and echo
All weathers that rattle
The windows, bang the door:
A storm contained, hailstones
Melting on this diaphragm.

Whistle

Cupped hands unfolding
A flutter of small wings
And fingers a diamond
Would be too heavy for,
Like ice that snares the feet
Of such dawn choruses
And prevents the robin
Ripening on its branch.

Pipes

One stool for the fireside
And the field, for windbag
And udder: milk and rain
Singing into a bucket
At the same angle: cries
Of waterbirds homing:
Ripples and undertow –
The chanter, the drones.

FERRY

I loop around this bollard
The beeline of cormorants,
The diver's shifts in air
And secure my idea
Of the island: rigging

Slanted across the sky,
Then a netting of sunlight
Where the thin oar splashes,
Stone steps down to the water
And a forgotten ferry.

FURY

On his mother's flank
A twist of blood, straw
Trailing to his crib
Behind the milk churns,

In the high rafters
Martins that chatter
Above his silence,
The white of his eye,

His enormous head's
Dithering acceptance
Of a breach birth,
A difficult name.

Somewhere already
The hiss of scythes,
The forking of hay
For his bony frame,

Over laid grasses
And thistles crows
Hustling to pin down
The new evictions.

I can just make out
His starry forehead
Hesitant among
Eyebright and speedwell.

TRUE STORIES
for Rebecca & Daniel

The Ring

I was ferried out to where
Petrels flung from the cliff face
Their long bodies, and underfoot
Plovers piled on pebbles
More pebbles, speckled eggs,

Four segments to each circle
Which I half-inscribed for you
By echoing both your names
And by fastening my ring
Around a fledgling's leg.

The Egg
for Daniel

It was your birth over again
Happening in my head as I let
Unfold in the palm of my hand
A tiny squeaking, a skull, feet,
Wings that the shell had compressed,

Yours the fulmar's exquisite eye
Balancing above one clean egg
And taking in all of the island,
The solitary snow goose, whiteness,
Bird lime among the sea campions.

The Nest

Next door to the tussocky well
I uncovered the lark's snug nest,
Our orderly neighbour: enough
To occupy you while you slept
Warming the eggs and silencing

The mallard's waterlogged alarum
From the bog, who, to spite the heron
And deflect a dangerous sky,
Had fouled her nest before leaving
And stained the immaculate shells.

The Wren
for Rebecca

After your two nightmares
(One about a giant bird
Lowering itself from the sky:
In the other both your eyes
Grew featureless as eggshells)

You were first to discover
A wren trapped in the kitchen:
Two pulses fluttering until
You had opened the window
On broken dreams, true stories.

HALCYON

Grandmother's plumage was death
To the few remaining grebes,
The solitary kingfisher
That haunted a riverbank.

But, then, I consider her
The last of the Pearly Queens
To walk under tall feathers –
The trophies of sweethearts

Who aimed from leafy towpaths
Pistols, silver bullets,
Or sank among bulrushes
Laying out nets of silk.

So many trigger fingers
And hands laid upon water
Should let materialise
A bird that breeds in winter,

That settles bad weather,
The winds of sickness and death –
Halcyon to the ancients
And kingfisher in those days,

Though perhaps even she knew
It was the eccentric grebe
Whose feet covered the surface,
Whose nest floated on the waves.

STILTS

for Paul Muldoon

Two grandfathers sway on stilts
Past my bedroom window.
They should be mending holes
In the Big Top, but that would be
Like putting out the stars.

The first has been a teacher
Of ballroom dancing, but now
Abandons house and home
To lift in the Grand Parade
High knees above the neighbours.

The second, a carpenter,
Comes from another town
With tools and material
To manufacture stilts
And playthings for the soul.

MASTER OF CEREMONIES

My grandfather, a natural master of ceremonies
('Boys! Girls! Take your partners for the Military Two-step!')
Had thrown out his only son, my sad retarded uncle
Who, good for nothing except sleepwalking to the Great War,
Was not once entrusted with rifle or bayonet but instead
Went over the top slowly behind the stretcher parties
And, as park attendant where all hell had broken loose,
Collected littered limbs until his sack was heavy.
In old age my grandfather demoted his flesh and blood
And over the cribbage board ('Fifteen two, fifteen four,
One for his nob') would call me Lionel. 'Sorry. My mistake.
That was my nephew. His head got blown off in No Man's Land.'

EDWARD THOMAS'S WAR DIARY

1 January – 8 April, 1917

One night in the trenches
You dreamed you were at home
And couldn't stay to tea,
Then woke where shell holes
Filled with bloodstained water,

Where empty beer bottles
Littered the barbed wire – still
Wondering why there sang
No thrushes in all that
Hazel, ash and dogwood,

Your eye on what remained –
Light spangling through a hole
In the cathedral wall
And the little conical
Summer house among trees.

Green feathers of yarrow
Were just fledging the sods
Of your dugout when you
Skirted the danger zone
To draw panoramas,

To receive larks singing
Like a letter from home
Posted in No Man's Land
Where one frantic bat seemed
A piece of burnt paper.

MOLE

Does a mole ever get hit by a shell?
Edward Thomas in his diary, 25.2.17

Who bothers to record
This body digested
By its own saliva
Inside the earth's mouth
And long intestine,

Or thanks it for digging
Its own grave, darkness
Growing like an eyelid
Over the eyes, hands
Swimming in the soil?

LOAMSHIRE

For years its economy has been running down
Because most of the inhabitants are poets
Who cultivate wild thyme or bog asphodel
And profess a diminishing interest in
The hidden meaning of the root vegetable.

The population explosion makes matters worse
Despite the by now famous last words of one
Who was crushed to death under his first tractor,
Or the demise of another who was kicked into
Unconsciousness for ever by a horse's hoof:

They both died smiling: and now the empty stable
That accumulates an aura of picturesque
Dilapidation, and the broken machinery
That drops petals of rust on to the relics, stand
As the shrines of a continuous pilgrimage.

Religious practice requires the sentimental
Sacrifice and complete extermination of
Such domestic animals as the pig and goat,
So that the prevalent diet has become
Badger hams, the occasional roast hedgehog,

Or, when in season, brightly coloured berries
And the unprotected eggs of rare species
Whose short memories return every springtime,
Risking naked eyes and hungry binoculars
To nest among denuded hedgerows, bare branches.

In all likelihood the number of emigrants
Would increase were it not for the sad tendency
Of the highways to dwindle to grassy byways
That meander beyond inaccurate signposts,
And the impossibility of locating,

Even if this were desirable, the county
Capital or some administrative centre
That might focus the scatter of smallholdings
And reduce the raggedly drawn boundary
To a dispute of international proportions.

FLEANCE

I entered with a torch before me
And cast my shadow on the backcloth
Momentarily: a handful of words,
One bullet with my initials on it –
And that got stuck in a property tree.

I would have caught it between my teeth
Or, a true professional, stood still
While the two poetic murderers
Pinned my silhouette to history
In a shower of accurate daggers.

But as any illusionist might
Unfasten the big sack of darkness,
The ropes and handcuffs, and emerge
Smoking a nonchalant cigarette,
I escaped – only to lose myself.

It took me a lifetime to explore
The dusty warren beneath the stage
With its trapdoor opening on to
All that had happened above my head
Like noises-off or distant weather.

In the empty auditorium I bowed
To one preoccupied caretaker
And, without removing my make-up,
Hurried back to the digs where Banquo
Sat up late with a hole in his head.

MAN LYING ON A WALL

Homage to L. S. Lowry

You could draw a straight line from the heels,
Through calves, buttocks and shoulderblades
To the back of the head: pressure points
That bear the enormous weight of the sky.
Should you take away the supporting structure
The result would be a miracle or
An extremely clever conjuring trick.
As it is, the man lying on the wall
Is wearing the serious expression
Of popes and kings in their final slumber,
His deportment not dissimilar to
Their stiff, reluctant exits from this world
Above the shoulders of the multitude.

It is difficult to judge whether or not
He is sleeping or merely disinclined
To arrive punctually at the office
Or to return home in time for his tea.
He is wearing a pinstripe suit, black shoes
And a bowler hat: on the pavement
Below him, like a relic or something
He is trying to forget, his briefcase
With everybody's initials on it.

ARS POETICA

I

Because they are somewhere in the building
I'll get in touch with them, the wife and kids –
Or I'm probably a widower by now,
Divorced and here by choice, on holiday
And paying through the nose for it: a queue
Of one outside the bathroom for ever
And no windows with a view of the sea.

II

I am writing a poem at the office desk
Or else I am forging business letters –
What I am really up to, I suspect,
Is seducing the boss's secretary
Among the ashtrays on the boardroom table
Before absconding with the petty-cash box
And a one-way ticket to Katmandu.

III

I go disguised as myself, my own beard
Changed by this multitude of distortions
To stage whiskers, my hair a give-away,
A cheap wig, and my face a mask only –
So that, on entering the hall of mirrors
The judge will at once award the first prize
To me and to all of my characters.

IV

After I've flown my rickety bi-plane
Under the Arc de Triomphe and before
I perform a double back-somersault
Without the safety net and – if there's time –
Walk the high wire between two waterfalls,
I shall draw a perfect circle free-hand
And risk my life in a final gesture.

V

Someone keeps banging the side of my head
Who is well aware that it's his furore,
His fists and feet I most want to describe –
My silence to date neither invitation
Nor complaint, but a stammering attempt
Once and for all to get him down in words
And allow him to push an open door.

VI

I am on general release now, having
Put myself in the shoes of all husbands,
Dissipated my substance in the parlours
Of an entire generation and annexed
To my territory gardens, allotments
And the desire – even at this late stage –
To go along with the world and his wife.

COMPANY

I imagine a day when the children
Are drawers full of soft toys, photographs
Beside the only surviving copies
Of the books that summarise my lifetime,
And I have begun to look forward to
Retirement, second childhood, except that
Love has diminished to one high room
Below which the vigilantes patrol
While I attempt to make myself heard
Above the cacophonous plumbing, and you
Who are my solitary interpreter
Can bear my company for long enough
To lipread such fictions as I believe
Will placate remote customs officials,
The border guards, or even reassure
Anxious butchers, greengrocers, tradesmen
On whom we depend for our daily bread,
The dissemination of manuscripts,
News from the outside world, simple acts
Of such unpatriotic generosity
That until death we hesitate together
On the verge of an almost total silence:

Or else we are living in the country
In a far-off townland divided by
The distances it takes to overhear
A quarrel or the sounds of love-making,
Where even impoverished households
Can afford to focus binoculars
On our tiny windows, the curtains
That wear my motionless silhouette

As I sit late beside a tilley-lamp
And try to put their district on the map
And to name the fields for them, for you
Who busy yourself about the cottage,
Its thatch letting in, the tall grasses
And the rain leaning against the half-door,
Dust on the rafters and our collection
Of curious utensils, pots and pans
The only escape from which is the twice
Daily embarrassed journey to and from
The well we have choked with alder branches
For the cattle's safety, their hoofprints
A thirsty circle in the puddles,
Watermarks under all that we say.

LAST RITES

I

I keep my own death-watch:
Mine the disembodied eye
At the hole in my head,
That blinks, watches through
Judas-hatch, fontanel:

Thus, round the clock, the last
Rites again and again:
A chipped mug, a tin plate
And no one there but myself,
My own worst enemy.

II

They can put out the drag-net:
Squads of intelligent detectives
Won't discover the hairs of my beard
Lodged like bookmarks between the pages
In even the remotest library,

Or the hairs of my head unravelling
For some Ariadne along dark
Corridors and back into my head,
Or the truth of my body, its sperm
Outnumbering the women in the world.

IV

THE ECHO GATE
(1979)

for Michael Allen & Paul Muldoon

I have heard of an island
With only one house on it.
The gulls are at home there.
Our perpetual absence
Is a way of leaving
All the eggs unbroken
That litter the ground
Right up to its doorstep.

OBSEQUIES

They are proof-reading my obituary now
As I fall asleep in formalin and float
Just below the surface of death, mute
At the centre of my long obsequies.

Were they to queue up to hear me breathing
The chemicals, then head over heels
All my lovers would fall in love again,
For I am a big fish in the aquarium,

A saint whose bits and pieces separate
Into a dozen ceremonies, pyres
For hands that bedded down like Gandhi
With the untouchables, funerals for feet.

They have set my eyes like two diamonds
In the black velvet of another's head,
Bartered silver, gold from knuckle and tooth
To purchase some sustenance for the needy.

Meanwhile, back at the dissecting theatre,
Part of me waits to find in sinks and basins
A final ocean, tears, water from the tap,
Superstitious rivers to take me there.

OLIVER PLUNKETT

His Soul

When they cut off his head, the long whiskers
Went on growing, as if to fledge his soul
And facilitate its gradual departure.

So much of him was concentrated there
That, quite without his realising it,
They divided the body into four.

It amounted to more than a withdrawal
When the last drop of moisture had dispersed
And one by one the hairs fell from his chin,

For the fatty brain was shrivelling as well,
Leaving around itself enormous spaces
And accommodation for the likes of him.

His own leathery shrine, he seems to be
Refracting the gleam in his father's eye
Like a shattered mirror in a handbag.

His Head

This is the end of the body that thinks
And says things, says things as the body does –
Kisses, belches, sighs – while making room for
The words of wisdom and the testimonies.

And these are a baby's features, a child's
Expression condensing on the plate glass,
The specimen suspended in its bottle
At eye level between shelf and shelf.

His head looks out from the tiny coffin
As though his body were crouching there
Inside the altar, a magician
Who is in charge of this conjuring trick,

Or an astronaut trapped by his oxygen
And eager to float upwards to the ceiling
Away from the gravitational pull
Of his arms and legs which are very old.

Your own face is reflected by the casket
And this is anybody's head in a room
Except that the walls are all windows and
He has written his name over the glass.

His Body

Trying to estimate what height he was
Keeps the soul awake, like the pea under
The heap of mattresses under the princess.

And now that they've turned him into a saint
Even a fly buzzing about the roof space
Must affect the balance of his mind.

His thigh bones and shoulder blades are scales
That a speck of dust could tilt, making him
Walk with a limp or become a hunchback.

He has been buried under the fingernails
Of his executioners, until they too fade
Like the lightning flash of their instruments.

There accompanies him around the cathedral
Enough silence to register the noise
Of the hairs on arms and legs expiring.

WREATHS

The Civil Servant

He was preparing an Ulster Fry for breakfast
When someone walked into the kitchen and shot him:
A bullet entered his mouth and pierced his skull,
The books he had read, the music he could play.

He lay in his dressing gown and pyjamas
While they dusted the dresser for fingerprints
And then shuffled backwards across the garden
With notebooks, cameras and measuring tapes.

They rolled him up like a red carpet and left
Only a bullet hole in the cutlery drawer:
Later his widow took a hammer and chisel
And removed the black keys from his piano.

The Greengrocer

He ran a good shop, and he died
Serving even the death-dealers
Who found him busy as usual
Behind the counter, organised
With holly wreaths for Christmas,
Fir trees on the pavement outside.

Astrologers or three wise men
Who may shortly be setting out
For a small house up the Shankill
Or the Falls, should pause on their way
To buy gifts at Jim Gibson's shop,
Dates and chestnuts and tangerines.

Christ's teeth ascended with him into heaven:
Through a cavity in one of his molars
The wind whistles: he is fastened for ever
By his exposed canines to a wintry sky.

I am blinded by the blaze of that smile
And by the memory of my father's false teeth
Brimming in their tumbler: they wore bubbles
And, outside of his body, a deadly grin.

When they massacred the ten linen workers
There fell on the road beside them spectacles,
Wallets, small change, and a set of dentures:
Blood, food particles, the bread, the wine.

Before I can bury my father once again
I must polish the spectacles, balance them
Upon his nose, fill his pockets with money
And into his dead mouth slip the set of teeth.

LAST REQUESTS

I

Your batman thought you were buried alive,
Left you for dead and stole your pocket watch
And cigarette case, all he could salvage
From the grave you so nearly had to share
With an unexploded shell. But your lungs
Surfaced to take a long remembered drag,
Heart contradicting as an epitaph
The two initials you had scratched on gold.

II

I thought you blew a kiss before you died,
But the bony fingers that waved to and fro
Were asking for a Woodbine, the last request
Of many soldiers in your company,
The brand you chose to smoke for forty years
Thoughtfully, each one like a sacrament.
I who brought peppermints and grapes only
Couldn't reach you through the oxygen tent.

SECOND SIGHT

My father's mother had the second sight.
Flanders began at the kitchen window –
The mangle rusting in No Man's Land, gas
Turning the antimacassars yellow
When it blew the wrong way from the salient.

In bandages, on crutches, reaching home
Before his letters, my father used to find
The front door on the latch, his bed airing.
'I watched my son going over the top.
He was carrying flowers out of the smoke.'

I have brought the *Pocket Guide to London,*
My *Map of the Underground,* an address –
A lover looking for somewhere to live,
A ghost among ghosts of aunts and uncles
Who crowd around me to give directions.

Where is my father's house, where my father?
If I could walk in on my grandmother
She'd see right through me and the hallway
And the miles of cloud and sky to Ireland.
'You have crossed the water to visit me.'

HOME GROUND

I
for S.H.

This was your home ground, comings and goings
When the sand martins collected in flight
Feathers and straw for untidy chambers
Or swooped up to kiss each tiny darkness,
Five white eggs changing to five white chins:

Childhood, and your townland poor enough
For gentians, fairy-flax, wild strawberries
And the anxious lapwing that settled there,
Its vocal cords a grass blade stretched
Between your thumbs and blown to tatters.

II
for P.M.

When they landed the first man on the moon
You were picking strawberries in a field,
Straggly fuses, lamps that stained the ground
And lips and fingers with reflected light,
For you were living then from hand to mouth.

Re-entering that atmosphere, you take
The dangerous bend outside the graveyard
Where your mother falls like a meteor
From clouds of may and damson blossom:
There the moon-rocks ripen in your hand.

ARCHITECTURE

The House on the Seashore

Laying down sand and shingle for the floor
And thatching with seaweed the low boulders
You make an echo-chamber of your home
That magnifies the wind to a cyclone
And keeps you from standing head and shoulders
Above the sea's whisper and the seashore.

The House Shaped Like an Egg

Do you pay for this house with egg money
Since its whitewashed walls are clean as shell
And the parlour, scullery, bedrooms oval
To leave no corner for dust or devil
Or the double yolk of heaven and hell
Or days when it rains and turns out sunny?

The House on the Bleach Green

This stump of a tree without any leaves
Can be occupied but never lived in
When snow is lying on the bleach green
And the smallest house you have ever seen
Lets someone inside to watch the linen
From tiny windows with a view of thieves.

The House Made out of Turf

Are the hearth and the chimney built of stone
Or can there be a fireplace for the fire
In a house made out of turf, with its roof
Of kindling, gables that may waterproof
This spacious tinderbox to make a pyre
Of what you built and heated on your own?

ASH KEYS

Ghosts of hedgers and ditchers,
The ash trees rattling keys
Above tangles of hawthorn
And bramble, alder and gorse,

Would keep me from pacing
Commonage, long perspectives
And conversations, a field
That touches the horizon.

I am herding cattle there
As a boy, as the old man
Following in his footsteps
Who begins the task again,

As though there'd never been
In some interim or hollow
Wives and children, milk
And buttermilk, market days.

Far from the perimeter
Of watercress and berries,
In the middle of the field
I stand talking to myself,

While the ash keys scatter
And the gates creak open
And the barbed wire rusts
To hay-ropes strung with thorns.

SPRING TIDE

I

I seem lower than the distant waves,
Their roar diluting to the stillness
Of the sea's progression across these flats,
A map of water so adjusted
It behaves like a preservative
And erases neither the cattle's
And the sheep's nor my own footprints.
I leave hieroglyphics under glass
As well as feathers that hardly budge,
Down abandoned at preening places
That last so long as grassy islands
Where swans unravel among the ferns.

II

It isn't really a burial mound
Reflected there, but all that remains
Of a sandy meadow, a graveyard
Where it was easy to dig the graves.
The spring tide circles and excavates
A shrunken ramshackle pyramid
Rinsing cleaner scapulae, tibias,
Loose teeth, cowrie and nautilus shells
Before seeping after sun and moon
To pour cupfuls into the larks' nests,
To break a mirror on the grazing
And lift minnows over the low bridge.

III

The spring tide has ferried jelly fish
To the end of the lane, pinks, purples,
Wet flowers beside the floating cow-pats.
The zig-zags I make take me among
White cresses and brookweed, lousewort,
Water plantain and grass of parnassus
With engraved capillaries, ivory sheen:
By a drystone wall in the dune slack
The greenish sepals, the hidden blush
And a lip's red veins and yellow spots –
Marsh helleborine waiting for me
To come and go with the spring tide.

ENTOMOLOGY

I

A dinner service becoming mouths
With just one snorkel above the bog,
The sundew puts out roots into the air,
Improves its hungry house by taking in
Passers-by, midges, mayflies, prisoners
Digested by their handcuffs and chains.

II

To catch butterflies in a butterfly net
Is to sense the unfolding of a shroud,
Is to count the many changes of skin
And the chances of being born again,
Is to waken up after sleeping in.
Even their eggs are built with little doors.

FROZEN RAIN

I slow down the waterfall to a chandelier,
Filaments of daylight, bones fleshed out by ice
That recuperate in their bandages of glass
And, where the lake behaves like a spirit-level,
I save pockets of air for the otter to breathe.

I magnify each individual blade of grass
With frozen rain, a crop of icicles and twigs,
Fingers and thumbs that beckon towards the thaw
And melt to the marrow between lip and tongue
While the wind strikes the branches like a celeste.

THAW

Snow curls into the coalhouse, flecks the coal.
We burn the snow as well in bad weather
As though to spring-clean that darkening hole.
The thaw's a blackbird with one white feather.

THE ECHO GATE

I stand between the pillars of the gate,
A skull between two ears that reconstructs
Broken voices, broken stones, history

And the first words that come into my head
Echoing back from the monastery wall
To measure these fields at the speed of sound.

LORE

Cutting the Last Sheaf

Divide into three braids the thickest clump of corn
Plaiting it like hair, tying it below the ears
To make sure that the harvest will not unravel,

Then, as though to hone them sharper upon the wind
Throw sickles until the last sheaf has been severed
And give it to a woman or a mare in foal.

Fishing for Sand Eels

They are hungry enough to fish for eels,
Sand eels, except that it's hardly fishing
To parade so slowly between the tides,

To be one of the moonlit multitude,
To slice sand and sea with a blunt sickle
Lest the harvest bleed when it is cut.

Working the Womenfolk

The man who would like his wife to dig in the fields
Will have to attach a wooden peg to her hoe,
Then cover her feet, and not with stockings only,

And do his bit at the milking stool and the churn
And even keep an eye on the wandering hen
For fear she might be laying in the nettle patch.

Bringing in the Kelp

There are even more fields under the sea
As though waves washed over a remote farm
And lanes extended there for cart or raft,

As though the handles of rake and sickle
Grew much longer in order to harvest
The salty tangle from those deep waters.

Ploughing by the Tail

Whoever plucks wool in thrifty skeins from his sheep
And bleeds his bull through a small hole in the neck
And blows into his cow to make her give more milk,

Is likely to do without a halter and reins
And plough by the tail, if the hairs are strong enough
And he has learned to tie the complicated knot.

Finding a Remedy

Sprinkle the dust from a mushroom or chew
The white end of a rush, apply the juice
From fern roots, stems of burdock, dandelions,

Then cover the wound with cuckoo-sorrel
Or sphagnum moss, bringing together verse
And herb, plant and prayer to stop the bleeding.

ON HEARING IRISH SPOKEN

Gliding together in a tidal shimmer to talk
Two fishermen leave behind another currach
Upturned on the beach, a hand cupped to an ear,

An echo of technical terms, the one I know
Repeating itself at desperate intervals
Like the stepping stones across a river in spate.

BOTANY

Duckweed

Afloat on their own reflection, these leaves
With roots that reach only part of the way,
Will fall asleep at the end of summer,
Draw in their skirts and sink to the bottom.

Foxglove

Though the corolla dangles upside down,
Nothing ever falls out, neither nectar
Nor loosening pollen grains: a thimble,
Stall for the little finger and the bee.

Dock

Its green flowers attract only the wind
But a red vein may irrigate the leaf
And blossom into blush or birthmark
Or a remedy for the nettle's sting.

Orchid

The tuber absorbs summer and winter,
Its own ugly shape, twisted arms and legs,
A recollection of the heart, one artery
Sprouting upwards to support a flower.

MAYO MONOLOGUES

Brothers

I was a mother and a father to him
Once his pebble spectacles had turned cloudy
And his walk slowed to a chair by the fire.
Often I would come back from herding sheep
Or from the post office with our pensions
To find his darkness in darkness, the turf
Shifting ashes on to last flakes of light.
The room was made more silent by the flies
That circled the soup stains on his waistcoat.
The dog preferred to curl up under his hand
And raced ahead as soon as I neared the lane.
I read to him from one of his six books,
Thick pages dropping from the broken spines
Of *Westward Ho!* and *The Children's Reciter.*
Sometimes I pulled faces, and he didn't know,
Or I paraded naked in front of him
As though I was looking in a mirror.
Two neighbours came visiting after he died.
Mad for the learning, a character, they said
And awakened in me a pride of sorts.
I picture his hand when I stroke the dog,
His legs if I knock the kettle from the hearth.
It's his peculiar way of putting things
That fills in the spaces of Thallabaun.
The dregs stewed in the teapot remind me,
And wind creaming rainwater off the butt.

Housekeeper

She burst out laughing at the interview
Because he complained about his catheter.
I had come from the far end of the county
To nurse his lordship and, when he died, stayed on.
Every morning here I have been surprised
By the stream that flows in the wrong direction.
I miss a mountain at the kitchen window.
The house is shrinking slowly to a few rooms
Where for longer periods she hides away
And sits arguing with herself, a hare
That chews over its droppings in the form.
I have caught her reading my letters home,
Hiding Christmas cards behind the piano.
She makes jokes to the friendly gardener
About my whiskery chin, my varicose veins,
And tells me off like a child in front of him
Should my fingernails be stained or floury.
If I start to talk about going home
She pretends not to understand my accent.
The bell that summons the afternoon tray
Will soon be ringing out for a bed pan.
Furniture and ornaments seem to linger
And wait under dust sheets for her to die.
A last sheet will cover up her armchair
And the hare that melts into the mountainside
Will be white in winter and eating snow.

Self-heal

I wanted to teach him the names of flowers,
Self-heal and centaury; on the long acre
Where cattle never graze, bog asphodel.
Could I love someone so gone in the head
And, as they say, was I leading him on?
He'd slept in the cot until he was twelve
Because of his babyish ways, I suppose,
Or the lack of a bed: hadn't his father
Gambled away all but rushy pasture?
His skull seemed to be hammered like a wedge
Into his shoulders, and his back was hunched,
Which gave him an almost scholarly air.
But he couldn't remember the things I taught:
Each name would hover above its flower
Like a butterfly unable to alight.
That day I pulled a cuckoo-pint apart
To release the giddy insects from their cell.
Gently he slipped his hand between my thighs.
I wasn't frightened; and still I don't know why,
But I ran from him in tears to tell them.
I heard how every day for one whole week
He was flogged with a blackthorn, then tethered
In the hayfield. I might have been the cow
Whose tail he would later dock with shears,
And he the ram tangled in barbed wire
That he stoned to death when they set him free.

Arrest

The sergeant called me by my christian name
And waited an hour while I tidied up.
Not once did he mention why he had come
Or when and where he would take me away.
He just moved quietly from wall to wall
As I swept the floor towards the flagstones
And leaned brush and shovel, the broken tongs
Next to the spade and hoe I'd brought inside.
I emptied the half-used packet of tea
Into the caddy and dusted the lid.
In the leaky basin with its brown ring
I washed knife, fork, spoon, the two teacups
And the saucer that does for an ashtray.
I put back the stools where they usually stand,
Hung the towel to dry over one of them
And spread fresh newspapers on the table.
When I'd thrown the water from the basin
I turned it upside down on the turf stack,
Then I packed my shaving brush and razor
And smoored the fire as though I might return.
They have locked me up in the institute
Because I made love to the animals.
I'd sooner stand barefoot, without a cap
And take in my acres from a distance,
From the rocky hilltops or the seashore,
From the purgatory of the windy gaps.

PEACE

after Tibullus

Who was responsible for the very first arms deal –
The man of iron who thought of marketing the sword?
Or did he intend us to use it against wild animals
Rather than ourselves? Even if he's not guilty
Murder got into the bloodstream as gene or virus
So that now we give birth to wars, short cuts to death.
Blame the affluent society: no killings when
The cup on the dinner table was made of beechwood,
And no barricades or ghettos when the shepherd
Snoozed among sheep that weren't even thoroughbreds.

I would like to have been alive in the good old days
Before the horrors of modern warfare and warcries
Stepping up my pulse rate. Alas, as things turn out
I've been press-ganged into service, and for all I know
Someone's polishing a spear with my number on it.
God of my Fathers, look after me like a child!
And don't be embarrassed by this handmade statue
Carved out of bog oak by my great-great-grandfather
Before the mass-production of religious art
When a wooden god stood simply in a narrow shrine.

A man could worship there with bunches of early grapes,
A wreath of whiskery wheat-ears, and then say Thank you
With a wholemeal loaf delivered by him in person,
His daughter carrying the unbroken honeycomb.
If the good Lord keeps me out of the firing line
I'll pick a porker from the steamy sty and dress
In my Sunday best, a country cousin's sacrifice.
Someone else can slaughter enemy commanders
And, over a drink, rehearse with me his memoirs,
Mapping the camp in wine upon the table top.

It's crazy to beg black death to join the ranks
Who dogs our footsteps anyhow with silent feet –
No cornfields in Hell, nor cultivated vineyards,
Only yapping Cerberus and the unattractive
Oarsman of the Styx: there an anaemic crew
Sleepwalks with smoky hair and empty eye-sockets.
How much nicer to have a family and let
Lazy old age catch up on you in your retirement,
You keeping track of the sheep, your son of the lambs,
While the woman of the house puts on the kettle.

I want to live until the white hairs shine above
A pensioner's memories of better days. Meanwhile
I would like peace to be my partner on the farm,
Peace personified: oxen under the curved yoke;
Compost for the vines, grape-juice turning into wine,
Vintage years handed down from father to son;
Hoe and ploughshare gleaming, while in some dark corner
Rust keeps the soldier's grisly weapons in their place;
The labourer steering his wife and children home
In a hay cart from the fields, a trifle sozzled.

Then, if there are skirmishes, guerrilla tactics,
It's only lovers quarrelling, the bedroom door
Wrenched off its hinges, a woman in hysterics,
Hair torn out, cheeks swollen with bruises and tears –
Until the bully-boy starts snivelling as well
In a pang of conscience for his battered wife:
Then sexual neurosis works them up again
And the row escalates into a war of words.
He's hard as nails, made of sticks and stones, the chap
Who beats his girlfriend up. A crime against nature.

Enough, surely, to rip from her skin the flimsiest
Of negligees, ruffle that elaborate hair-do,
Enough to be the involuntary cause of tears –
Though upsetting a sensitive girl when you sulk
Is a peculiar satisfaction. But punch-ups,
Physical violence, are out: you might as well
Pack your kit-bag, goose-step a thousand miles away
From the female sex. As for me, I want a woman
To come and fondle my ears of wheat and let apples
Overflow between her breasts. I shall call her Peace.

THE WAR POETS

Unmarked were the bodies of the soldier-poets
For shrapnel opened up again the fontanel
Like a hailstone melting towards deep water
At the bottom of a well, or a mosquito
Balancing its tiny shadow above the lip.

It was rushes of air that took the breath away
As though curtains were drawn suddenly aside
And darkness streamed into the dormitory
Where everybody talked about the war ending
And always it would be the last week of the war.

BOG COTTON

Let me make room for bog cotton, a desert flower –
Keith Douglas, I nearly repeat what you were saying
When you apostrophised the poppies of Flanders
And the death of poetry there: that was in Egypt
Among the sandy soldiers of another war.

(It hangs on by a thread, denser than thistledown,
Reluctant to fly, a weather vane that traces
The flow of cloud shadow over monotonous bog –
And useless too, though it might well bring to mind
The plumpness of pillows, the staunching of wounds,

Rags torn from a petticoat and soaked in water
And tied to the bushes around some holy well
As though to make a hospital of the landscape –
Cures and medicines as far as the horizon
Which nobody harvests except with the eye.)

You saw that beyond the thirstier desert flowers
There fell hundreds of thousands of poppy petals
Magnified to blood stains by the middle distance
Or through the still unfocused sights of a rifle –
And Isaac Rosenberg wore one behind his ear.

SULPICIA

Round this particular date I have drawn a circle
For Mars, dressed myself up for him, dressed to kill:
When I let my hair down I am a sheaf of wheat
And I bring in the harvest without cutting it.

Were he to hover above me like a bird of prey
I would lay my body out, his little country,
Fields smelling of flowers, flowers in the hedgerow –
And then I would put on an overcoat of snow.

I will stumble behind him through the undergrowth
Tracking his white legs, drawing about us both
The hunters' circle: among twisted nets and snares

I will seduce him, tangle his hairs with my hairs
While the stag dashes off on one of its tangents
And boars root safely along our circumference.

FLORENCE NIGHTINGALE

Through your pocket glass you have let disease expand
To remote continents of pain where you go far
With rustling cuff and starched apron, a soft hand:
Beneath the bandage maggots are stitching the scar.

For many of the men who lie there it is late
And you allow them at the edge of consciousness
The halo of your lamp, a brothel's fanlight
Or a nightlight carried in by nanny and nurse.

You know that even with officers and clergy
Moustachioed lips will purse into fundaments
And under sedation all the bad words emerge
To be rinsed in your head like the smell of wounds,

Death's vegetable sweetness at both rind and core –
Name a weed and you find it growing everywhere.

GRACE DARLING

After you had steered your coble out of the storm
And left the smaller islands to break the surface,
Like draughts shaking that colossal backcloth there came
Fifty pounds from the Queen, proposals of marriage.

The daughter of a lighthouse-keeper and the saints
Who once lived there on birds' eggs, rainwater, barley
And built to keep all pilgrims at a safe distance
Circular houses with views only of the sky,

Who set timber burning on the top of a tower
Before each was launched at last in his stone coffin –
You would turn your back on mainland and suitor
To marry, then bereave the waves from Lindisfarne,

A moth against the lamp that shines still and reveals
Many small boats at sea, lifeboats, named after girls.

MENISCUS

You are made out of water mostly, spittle, tears
And the blood that colours your cheek, red water.
Even your ears are ripples, your knuckles, knees
Damp stones that wear the meniscus like a skin.
Your breasts condense and adhere, drops of water.
And, where your body curves like a basin, faces
Are reflected, then dissolved by swaying water.

METAMORPHOSES

I

A boulder locked in a cranny,
A head without a face, she waits
For rain to hollow out a font
And fill her eye in, blink by blink.

II

She will be felled like timber
So that anyone may study
Clefts made by the highest branches,
The faces hidden in the bark.

III

She sleeps in ponds and puddles
And sinks to her own level,
A bed for watercress, water
Snuggling in its own embrace.

IV

Her legs are the roots of a tree
That have grown around a boulder
As though she might give birth to it
By pressing hard into the ground.

MARTINMAS

Not even ashes and the sweepings from the floor
Are to be thrown out, stray hairs of yours, flakes of skin,
For that would be digging a grave, burying someone
Before the weather mends and cold stones are lifted
From the river bed, the charred sticks from our hearth,
My sooty finger smudging your arm and forehead
As I leave to scatter grain into the furrows,
To wait with my sickle among the unripe stalks
Until the Feast of Saint Martin, you by my bed
Letting down your hair and weeping while you undress
Because you are the harvest I must gather in.
We grind the ears of corn to death between our bones.

MOUNTAIN SWIM

Hilltop and valley floor we sway between,
Our bodies sustained as by a hammock,
Our nakedness water stretched on stone,

One with the shepherd's distant whistle,
The hawk lifted on its thermal, the hare
Asleep in its excrement like a child.

ON MWEELREA

I

I was lowering my body on to yours
When I put my ear to the mountain's side
And eavesdropped on water washing itself
In the locked bath-house of the underground.

When I dipped my hand among hidden sounds
It was the water's pulse at wrist and groin,
It was the water that reminded me
To leave all of my jugs and cups behind.

II

The slopes of the mountain were commonage
For me clambering over the low walls
To look for the rings of autumn mushrooms
That ripple out across the centuries.

I had made myself the worried shepherd
Of snipe twisting the grasses into curls
And tiny thatches where they hid away,
Of the sheep that grazed your maidenhair.

III

September grew to shadows on Mweelrea
Once the lambs had descended from the ridge
With their fleeces dyed, tinges of sunset,
Rowan berries, and the bracken rusting.

Behind my eyelids I could just make out
In a wash of blood and light and water
Your body colouring the mountainside
Like uncut poppies in the stubbly fields.

THE LINEN INDUSTRY

Pulling up flax after the blue flowers have fallen
And laying our handfuls in the peaty water
To rot those grasses to the bone, or building stooks
That recall the skirts of an invisible dancer,

We become a part of the linen industry
And follow its processes to the grubby town
Where fields are compacted into window-boxes
And there is little room among the big machines.

But even in our attic under the skylight
We make love on a bleach green, the whole meadow
Draped with material turning white in the sun
As though snow reluctant to melt were our attire.

What's passion but a battering of stubborn stalks,
Then a gentle combing out of fibres like hair
And a weaving of these into christening robes,
Into garments for a marriage or funeral?

Since it's like a bereavement once the labour's done
To find ourselves last workers in a dying trade,
Let flax be our matchmaker, our undertaker,
The provider of sheets for whatever the bed –

And be shy of your breasts in the presence of death,
Say that you look more beautiful in linen
Wearing white petticoats, the bow on your bodice
A butterfly attending the embroidered flowers.

HOUSEHOLD HINTS

Old clothes have hearts, livers that last longer:
The veils, chemises, embroidered blouses
Brought back to life in suds and warm water,
Black lace revived by black tea, or crape
Passed to and fro through steam from a kettle.

So look on this as an antique nightdress
That has sleepwalked along hundreds of miles
Of rugs and carpets and linoleum,
Its clean hem lifted over the spilt milk
And ink, the occasional fall of soot.

This places you at a dressing-table,
Two sleeves that float into the looking-glass
Above combs and brushes, mother-of-pearl,
Tortoiseshell, silver, the discreet litter
Of your curling papers and crimping pins.

Though I picked it up for next to nothing
Wear this each night against your skin, accept
My advice about blood stains and mildew,
Cedar wood and camphor as protection
Against moths, alum-water against fire,

For I have been bruised like the furniture
And am more than a list of household hints,
The blackleader of stoves and bootscrapers,
Mender of sash cords, the mirror you slip
Between sheets to prove that the bed is damp.

DEAD MEN'S FINGERS

The second time we meet I am waiting in a pub
Beside the cigarette machine. She is in her moons.
A cat with a mouse's tail dangling out of its mouth
Flashes from between her legs and escapes into my head.
There follow trips to the seaside where I find for her
Feathers, shells, dune violets among the marram grass;

Then the conversational strolls in a forest of pines
So that I can picture the invisible tree-creeper
Spiralling up her body to probe for such parasites
As lurk where pink flowers seem to harden into cones.
Next comes that honeymoon weekend in a farflung cottage
Where we sit in silence and borrow light from the door,

And I boil a somnolent lobster in the ash bucket
And divide it between us. Our most memorable meal.
But surely she has eaten dead men's fingers by mistake
Because her sickness interrupts us like a telephone.
The tenth, eleventh, twelfth occasions melt together
Colourfully: a stained-glass window in a burning church.

Indeed, I soon find myself, wherever a fire is lit,
Crossing my legs, putting my feet up on the mantelpiece
And talking to my shoes, with glances in her direction.
The first time we meet is really the last time in reverse.
We kiss for ever and I feel like the ghost of a child
Visiting the mother who long ago aborted him.

THE BARBER'S WIFE

I seem to be the last customer
For blinds are drawn on instruments,

On combs and razors, clicking scissors,
Clippers that buzz among pomades.

As though everything depends on it
A drop of water clings to the tap,

A lens inverting the premises
Until the barber's wife appears.

Does she always come at five o'clock
To sweep the presences, absences,

Earthly remains, ghosts of skulls
With graceful movements into the bin?

She is an interloper, two eyes
Penetrating the back of my head.

Then I see that she repeats herself
In one mirror after another,

That the barber and I are eunuchs
In the harem of her reflections.

SELF-PORTRAIT

My great-great-grandfather fell in top hat and tails
Across the threshold, his cigar brightly burning
While the chalk outline they had traced around his body
Got up and strolled through the door and became me,

But not before his own son had wasted a lifetime
Waiting to be made Lord Mayor of the Universe.
He was to choke to death on a difficult word
When a food particle lodged against his uvula.

I came into being alongside a twin brother
Who threatened me at first like an abortionist
Recommending suicide jumps and gin with cloves.
Then he blossomed into my guardian angel.

Peering back to the people who ploughed the Long Field
My eyes are bog holes that reflect a foreign sky.
Moustaches thatch my utterance in such a way
That no one can lipread the words from a distance.

I am, you will have noticed, all fingers and thumbs
But, then, so is the wing of a bat, a bird's wing.
I articulate through the nightingale's throat,
Sing with the vocal cords of the orang-outang.

CODICILS

I

Your hands hold my neck and head
As though you were bathing me
Or lifting me out of darkness,
Hands that shelter a night-light,
Balance a spoon for medicine.

When you turn from me to sleep
A lamplighter on his bicycle
Will see you to the corner,
Gas mantles in his saddle bag,
Across his shoulder a long pole.

II

It is a last desolate weaning
When you hug me, the sole survivor
– Without location or protocol –
Of a tribe which let the fire go out.

I shall explain to the first stranger
With a smattering of my dialect
Why I am huddled up in mourning
And, like a baby, sucking my thumb.

V

POEMS
(1985)

I have been tapping the distances between us,
An engineer at his ease up a telegraph pole
Or a saboteur galvanised on the power lines,
Wedding ring and buttons soldered to his skin.

VIEW

I have put my arms around her skeleton
For fear that her forearms might unravel
Like hawsers, ligaments stiffening to kelp
That keeps ocean and boulders in their places,
Weights on the heart, ballast for the ribcage,
Stones to be lifted out of the currach
And arranged as a sundial where she points
To the same cottage on every island –
There's always a view over her shoulder.

PATCHWORK

I

There are ribbons that hold you together,
Hooks and eyes, hollows at the collarbone,

As though you dismantle your skeleton
Before stepping out of the crumpled ring,

Your nipples under my fingertips
Like white flowers on a white ground.

II

I pull up over us old clothes, remnants,
Stitching together shirts and nightshirts

Into such a dazzle as will burn away
Newspapers, letters, previous templates,

The hearth too, a red patch at the centre
That scorches the walls and our low ceiling.

LIGHT BEHIND THE RAIN

I

Come hugging your breasts
As if to comfort them,
Ripening in your armpit
Fingertip, knuckle-bone
And then, like a branch,
Canopy the windfalls.

II

You will reduce me to an eel
That drenches the stubble, inhales
The dew, a thorn in a puddle
Dimpling the water's membrane.

III

Implicate in your hair
Timorous featherbrains,
Headaches in the hedge,
Eggs warming and cooling
On cobwebs, thistledown,
White ones you pluck out.

IV

You have collected me into your hand
Now that the blackbird abandons the nest,
Yolks curdling beneath their porcelain,

A grave in the branches for wind and weeds
To cover up, and not the mother's breast,
The teepee she makes of bones and feathers.

V

From my belly or thigh
As love evaporates,
Lift with your fingernail
A flake of rice-paper,

Weigh what meat there is
On the shin of a wren,
The marrow full of air,
The feathers full of rain.

VI

My mouth reads into you
Light behind the rain,
Boulders beneath the soil,
Between breath and bone
Water gone underground.

VII

Where barley weighs the food in its hair
You materialise like a farmer's wife
Who last summer occupied the distance
– A sewing basket among the stooks –
And left me behind, trawling the milk
With goose-grass for strands of your hair.

VIII

You leave a moon at the window
And, as the lifeless nebulae
Sink beneath my sleeping hand,
Not one red vein in the sky.

MAGGIE MOORE'S

I am standing behind you in Maggie Moore's
Second-hand clothes shop in Sandy Row.
A single electric light bulb
Raises the bumps on the bumpy floor.
You rummage through crochet-work and cobwebs.

Moths flit out from the sweaty arm-holes
Of party frocks and summer dresses,
Nightdresses mothers and grandmothers wore.
As in a dream all take off their clothes
And vanish for ever down Sandy Row.

I am the guard who polishes his rifle
With a rag you recognise as silk
Or chiffon, perfect material
For you to embroider with designs
That cover and reveal your body.

And I am the young amazed GI
Passing rag after rag through barbed wire
And ripping the sleeve of his uniform.
He knows that your clothes are second-hand.
He brings down the shutters on Maggie Moore's.

LOVE POEM

When my fingers touch your body's
Sorrowing stubble, so young
You feel, so old, all I can see
Is an area with barbed wire
And an orphan squatting there.

It is nineteen forty, forty-one
Which makes him a sort of twin,
But he has never known a tree
And he does not laugh or cry
Or wait for your hairs to grow.

LOVE POET

I make my peace with murderers.
I lock pubic hair from victims
In an airtight tin, mummify
Angel feathers, tobacco shreds.

All that survives my acid bath
Is a solitary gall-stone
Like a pebble out on mud flats
Or the ghost of an avocado.

AMONG WATERBIRDS

Between us and the wind from the wetlands
There are no windbreaks but waterbirds' wings.

A duck egg balances, greeny-blue,
And eclipses the feathers of the sun.

You are my weather-sense, crests lifting –
Let me use your body like a hide.

MARKINGS

for Sarah

I

The markings almost disappear
With the shadowy sound you make
Launching the feather from your hand,
As though you would learn to whistle
By answering the curlew's cry.

II

I would remember tumblers
Above the water-meadow,
The shimmer of white feathers
In the flower-dwarfing wind,

Brood-patch and bird-brain,
The hummock of her body
That tries to make head or tail
Of movements inside the shell.

All that remains to show you
Is the deserted nest-bowl,
Blots and scribbles on an egg,
The dappled flight of lapwings.

III

One more pebble on the cairn
Might make it a vantage point
For the stonechat, a headstone
Should winter blow out his song,
His chestnut breast a tinderbox
Igniting the few syllables.

NO MAN'S LAND

in memory of Isaac Rosenberg

I

Who will give skin and bones to my Jewish granny?
She has come down to me in the copperplate writing
Of three certificates, a dog-eared daguerreotype
And the one story my grandfather told about her.

He tossed a brick through a rowdy neighbour's window
As she lay dying, and Jessica, her twenty years
And mislaid whereabouts gave way to a second wife,
A terrible century, a circle of christian names.

II

I tilt her head towards you, Isaac Rosenberg,
But can you pick out that echo of splintering glass
From under the bombardment, and in No Man's Land
What is there to talk about but difficult poems?

Because your body was not recovered either
I try to read the constellations of brass buttons,
Identity discs that catch the light a little.
A shell-shocked carrier pigeon flaps behind the lines.

HALLOWE'EN

It is Hallowe'en. Turnip Head
Will soon be given his face,
A slit, two triangles, a hole.
His brains litter the table top.
A candle stub will be his soul.

ON SLIEVE GULLION

for Douglas Carson

On Slieve Gullion 'men and mountain meet',
O'Hanlon's territory, the rapparee,
Home of gods, backdrop for a cattle raid,
The Lake of Cailleach Beara at the top
That slaked the severed head of Conor Mor:

To the south the Border and Ravensdale
Where the torturers of Nairac left
Not even an eyelash under the leaves
Or a tooth for MacCecht the cupbearer
To rinse, then wonder where the water went.

I watch now through a gap in the hazels
A blackened face, the disembodied head
Of a mummer who has lost his bearings
Or, from the garrison at Dromintee,
A paratrooper on reconnaissance.

He draws a helicopter after him,
His beret far below, a wine-red spot
Swallowed by heathery patches and ling
As he sweats up the slopes of Slieve Gullion
With forty pounds of history on his back.

Both strangers here, we pass in silence
For he and I have dried the lakes and streams
And Conor said too long ago: 'Noble
And valiant is MacCecht the cupbearer
Who brings water that a king may drink.'

SMOKE IN THE BRANCHES

The Disfigurement of Fergus

This is a scream no one will have heard
Bubbling up out of his mind, nightmare
Distorting his face on the sea-bed
To an ugliness that craves its mirror,
A watery death to cure and wash
The King of Ulster and his blemish.

The Grey of Macha

When big tears of blood roll down the face
Of the Grey of Macha, Cuchulain's horse,
They sprinkle the chariot and harness
That might as well be dragging a hearse
Over a battlefield slushy with brains,
Over the teeth like a shower of hailstones.

The Bewilderment of Muircertach

Muircertach mac Erca, King of Ireland,
Is waging war against fern and thistle,
Damaging pebbles, wounding the ground
Between life and death, grave and castle,
Where the woman he adores will vanish
Like a puffball or smoke in the branches.

The Death of Mac Glas

He isn't pulling a funny face
Although the Leinstermen laugh at him
Who, seconds ago, was only Mac Glas
The jester contriving another game,
While the entrails, tugged by a raven
Out of his wound, loop up to heaven.

THE THIRD LIGHT

The sexton is opening up the grave,
Lining with mossy cushions and couch grass
This shaft of light, entrance to the earth
Where I kneel to marry you again,
My elbows in darkness as I explore
From my draughty attic your last bedroom.
Then I vanish into the roof space.

I have handed over to him your pain
And your preference for Cyprus sherry,
Your spry quotations from the *Daily Mail*
With its crossword solved in ink, your limp
And pills, your scatter of cigarette butts
And last-minute humorous spring-cleaning
Of one corner of a shelf in his cupboard.

You spent his medals like a currency,
Always refusing the third light, afraid
Of the snipers who would extinguish it.
Waiting to scramble hand in hand with him
Out of the shell hole, did you imagine
A Woodbine passing to and fro, a face
That stabilises like a smoke ring?

THE WHITE BUTTERFLY

I wish that before you died
I had told you the legend,
A story from the Blaskets
About how the cabbage-white
May become the soul of one
Who lies sleeping in the fields.

Out of his mouth it wanders
And in through the eye-socket
Of an old horse's skull
To explore the corridors
And empty chamber, then
Flies back inside his lips.

This is a dream and flowers
Are bordering the journey
And the road leads on towards
That incandescent palace
Where from one room to the next
There is no one to be seen.

When I asked you as a child
How high should fences be
To keep in the butterflies,
Blood was already passing
Down median and margin
To the apex of a wing.

RUNE

Poems in the palm of the hand, life-lines,
Fingers tapping the ridge of the shin-bone,
The bridge of the nose, fingerprints, breath;
Then the silvery skin of the lifeless,
Ivy increasing the secrets, the answers –
The physician's power in cold dwellings,
Candles behind this veil of synonyms,
A blind man's lovely wife and signature.

A LAST ONE

in memory of Martin McBirney
& Brian O'Donnell

Stand me a last one for the road ahead,
Its roundabouts and lay-bys: no hurry when
The weather is dampening hearth and bed –
Making love in a house full of children,
Political arguments with the dead.

VI

GORSE FIRES
(1991)

In Memory of my Parents

Between now and one week ago when the snow fell, a bird landed
Where they lie, and made cosier and whiter the white patchwork:
And where I imagine her ashes settling on to his collarbone,
The tracks vanish between wing-tips symmetrically printed.

Shells I speak and light clouds, and a boat buds in the rain.
Paul Celan

SEA SHANTY

I would have waited under the statue of Eros
While the wind whistled in my bell-bottoms,
Taken my bearings from the blink of daylight
Her thighs and feathery maidenhair let through.
But now from the high ground of Carrigskeewaun
I watch Lesbos rising among the islands.
Rain shivers off the machair, and exposes me
In my long-johns, who dozed on her breastbone,
On pillows of sea-pink beyond the shingle,
Who mumbled into the ringlets at her ear
My repertoire of sea shanties and love songs.
I shake like a rock-fern, and my ill will
And smoky breath seem to wither the lichens.
I am making do with what has been left me,
The saltier leaves of samphire for my salad.
At midnight the moon goes, then the Pleiades,
A sparkle of sand grains on my wellingtons.

WASHING

All the washing on the line adds up to me alone.
When the cows go home and the golden plover calls
I bring it in, but leave pegged out at intervals
Dooaghtry Lake and David's Lake and Corragaun,
Gaps in the dunes, a sky-space for the lapwings
And the invisible whiteness of your underthings.

PHOSPHORESCENCE

There was light without heat between the stepping stones
And the duach, at every stride the Milky Way.
Her four or five petals hanging from an eyelash,
Venus bloomed like brookweed next to the Pleiades.

MIGRATIONS

I have hidden a key under the drystone wall
For lovers to make after me a home from home –
My gifts turf in a creel, buckets of lake water,
Their witnesses waders gathering for Greenland,
The Arctic, and pebbly nests below the snow-line.
I sleep on the other side of the hill from them.

MADAME BUTTERFLY

Through atmospherics I hear you die again.
Death is white as your lover's uniform, as snow
When it covers the whiteness of almond petals.
Worse weather blows your papery house away.
Now I listen for the snow bunting's arrival,
A flute-note from crevices and rocky scree.

BETWEEN HOVERS

in memory of Joe O'Toole

And not even when we ran over the badger
Did he tell me he had cancer, Joe O'Toole
Who was psychic about carburettor and clutch
And knew a folk cure for the starter-engine.
Backing into the dark we floodlit each hair
Like a filament of light our lights had put out
Somewhere between Kinnadoohy and Thallabaun.
I dragged it by two gritty paws into the ditch.
Joe spotted a ruby where the canines touched.
His way of seeing me safely across the duach
Was to leave his porch light burning, its sparkle
Shifting from widgeon to teal on Corragaun Lake.
I missed his funeral. Close to the stony roads
He lies in Killeen Churchyard over the hill.
This morning on the burial mound at Templedoomore
Encircled by a spring tide and taking in
Cloonaghmanagh and Claggan and Carrigskeewaun,
The townlands he'd wandered tending cows and sheep,
I watched a dying otter gaze right through me
At the islands in Clew Bay, as though it were only
Between hovers and not too far from the holt.

INSOMNIA

I could find my way to either lake at this late hour
Sleepwalking after the night-alarms of whooper swans.
If I get to sleep, the otter I have been waiting for
Will surface in the estuary near the stepping stones.

167

DETOUR

I want my funeral to include this detour
Down the single street of a small market town,
On either side of the procession such names
As Philbin, O'Malley, MacNamara, Keane.
A reverent pause to let a herd of milkers pass
Will bring me face to face with grubby parsnips,
Cauliflowers that glitter after a sunshower,
Then hay rakes, broom handles, gas cylinders.
Reflected in the slow sequence of shop windows
I shall be part of the action when his wife
Draining the potatoes into a steamy sink
Calls to the butcher to get ready for dinner
And the publican descends to change a barrel.
From behind the one locked door for miles around
I shall prolong a detailed conversation
With the man in the concrete telephone kiosk
About where my funeral might be going next.

OTTERS

I

As though it were the only one in Ireland
I lie above Corragaun and watch an otter
Tying and untying knots in the undertow
And wiring me like a harebell to the wind.

II

An upturned currach at Allaran Point
And a breaking wave are holt and hover
Until the otter, on wet sand in between,
Engraves its own reflection and departure.

PEREGRINE

I had been waiting for the peregrine falcon
As a way of coming to terms with the silence,
As a way of getting closer to you – an idea
Above the duach, downy whirlwinds, the wind's
Mother-of-pearl for instance, an eddy of bones.

Did the peregrine falcon when I was cycling
To meet you, swoop from the corner of my eye
And in and out of the culvert and out of sight
As though to avoid colliding with me – wings
Under the road, a blur of spokes and feathers?

PURLIN

Where there's nothing to fell but hazel scrub and hawthorn
You will need to disinter the wood to make your purlin,
Deciphering the slow gasses that, for thousands of years,
Have cast from underground the shadow of a tree-trunk
By keeping the frost away that soon will come over you
After you fall asleep in the roof-space, timber's grave.

IN AILLWEE CAVE

There must be grazing overhead, hazel thickets,
Pavements the rain is dissolving, springs and graves,
Darkness above the darkness of the seepage of souls
And hedges where goosegrass spills its creamy stars.

REMEMBERING CARRIGSKEEWAUN

A wintry night, the hearth inhales
And the chimney becomes a windpipe
Fluffy with soot and thistledown,
A voice-box recalling animals:
The leveret come of age, snipe
At an angle, then the porpoises'
Demonstration of meaningless smiles.
Home is a hollow between the waves,
A clump of nettles, feathery winds,
And memory no longer than a day
When the animals come back to me
From the townland of Carrigskeewaun,
From a page lit by the Milky Way.

GORSE FIRES

Cattle out of their byres are dungy still, lambs
Have stepped from last year as from an enclosure.
Five or six men stand gazing at a rusty tractor
Before carrying implements to separate fields.

I am travelling from one April to another.
It is the same train between the same embankments.
Gorse fires are smoking, but primroses burn
And celandines and white may and gorse flowers.

HOMECOMING

The brightest star came out, the day-star, dawn's star
And the seafaring ship drew near to Ithaca, to home
And that harbour named after the old man of the sea, two
Headlands huddling together as breakwater, windbreak,
Haven where complicated vessels float free of moorings
In their actual mooring-places.
                                    At the harbour-head
A long-leaved olive overshadows a shadowy cave
Full of bullauns, basins hollowed out of stone, stone
Jars for honey-bees, looms of stone on which are woven
Sea-purplish things – also, inextinguishable springs
And two ways in, one looking north where men descend
While the other faces south, a footpath for the gods.

When they had scrunched ashore at this familiar cove
And disembarked, they lifted Odysseus out of his hollow
Just as he was, linen sheet and glossy rug and all,
And put him to bed on the sand, still lost in sleep.

MERCURY

An inch above the horizon
Where the fields dip, Mercury
Seems to be reflecting Venus,
As though you were carrying
Through the gate a candle flame
And shielding it with your hand
For fear it might be put out
By the wind or the distance.

GOLDCREST

When you weighed against
A dried-out wine cork
The goldcrest, then buried
The twelfth of an ounce
Which was its eye, feathers
And inner workings,
Did you release, love,
Among the tree tops
The ghost of a bouquet?

THE VELOCIPEDE

He walks past my bedroom window carrying a spade.
That Joseph Murphy, father of four sets of twins,
Jockey, lover of horses, the gun club's secretary,
Should hide in his cottage a ledger full of poems
Is hardly surprising: consider his grandfather
Who beachcombed from the strand barrels and spars
And built the first velocipede in Thallabaun.
Out of an umbrella and old sheets he improvised
A parachute, launched himself from the byre roof
And after a brief flight was taken to hospital.
On home-made crutches and slipping all the tethers
Joseph Murphy's grandfather swings past my window.

HALLEY'S COMET

Homage to Erik Satie

It was the seventeenth variation after all.
The original theme had fluttered out of my hands
And upside down on the linoleum suggested it.
An ink blot on the stave inspired the modulation,
Or was it a bloodstain, a teardrop's immortality
Perfectly pitched between parallels, horizontals,
The provisional shorelines, amphibian swamps?
I got drunk on a pint mug full of white feathers.
I couldn't sleep because inside my left nostril
A hair kept buzzing with signals from Halley's comet
As it swung its skirt of heavenly dust particles
On a parabola around the electric light bulb.
This won't recur for another seventy-six years.

JUG BAND

in memory of Philip Larkin

We would follow that New Orleans marching band
As it passes the settee for the hundredth time,
But we have left clarinet and drums behind
And make up the instruments, and then the theme,

And the theme is the making up of instruments,
Jugs and kazoos for us to improvise our souls,
Thimbles for keeping time with and making sense
On a washboard of our uncomplicated roles.

THE SHACK

for Dillon & Guinn

I lie awake between the two sleeping couples.
Their careful breathing in the Blue Ridge Mountains
Disturbs me more than the engine ticking over
At the end of the lane, the repetitive whippoorwill,
The downpour's crescendo on corrugated iron.
Though there are no doors between them and me, perhaps
They will risk making love like embarrassed parents
While I remain motionless on my creaking divan.
They have shown me a copperhead, indian fire pinks
And buzzards like mobiles where the storm clouds hang.
I might as well be outside in the steamy field
Interrupting again the opossums' courtship,
Paralysing with torchlight pink noses, naked tails
Just beyond the shithouse where, like a fall of snow,
The equalising lime has covered our excrement.
Tomorrow when we pass the Pentecostal church
The wayside pulpit will read 'Thanks, Lord, for the rain.'

HUMMING BIRD

When a single sheet's too heavy and the night perspires
And the wild turkey cock blunders from the undergrowth,
I long for fast wings in the branches, the hesitations
Among these unknown flowers of my first humming bird.

QUAILS' EGGS

We listen for quails among ferns and twigs
And translate that call as 'wet-my-lips'.
Food–gatherers, eaters of quails' eggs
We throw our voices like ventriloquists.

AN AMISH RUG

As if a one-room schoolhouse were all we knew
And our clothes were black, our underclothes black,
Marriage a horse and buggy going to church
And the children silhouettes in a snowy field,

I bring you this patchwork like a smallholding
Where I served as the hired boy behind the harrow,
Its threads the colour of cantaloupe and cherry
Securing hay bales, corn cobs, tobacco leaves.

You may hang it on the wall, a cathedral window,
Or lay it out on the floor beside our bed
So that whenever we undress for sleep or love
We shall step over it as over a flowerbed.

IN A MISSISSAUGA GARDEN

The ghosts of the aunt and uncles I never knew
Put in an appearance when I meet my cousin.
Charlie, big in the Union, straightens his plus-fours.
Hugh is curing home-grown tobacco in the garage
While my grandparents lie upstairs, out of sorts.
Seamstress to the Court, Daisy burns a cigarette hole
In the chesterfield, then makes the tea for everyone.
Maurice keeps fiddling with the wind-up gramophone.
Having come all the way across the Atlantic
From Clapham Common to this Mississauga garden,
They flit out of sight like the different robins
Or the blackbird with flashes of red on its wings.

SWALLOW

When the swallow detoured into the kitchen
Kissing corners, highlighting the dusty shelves
With its underside, those exhausted feathers
That never quite made it through the open door,
We too were on the verge of moving house:

In the fridge a neglected rainbow trout,
A mouse mummifying underneath the piano,
Dead friends, draughts from the rafters, artisans
From the Land of Promise or thereabouts
Thatching with the wings of birds our house.

TREE-HOUSE

When he described how he had built the ingenious bedroom
Around that bushy olive-tree – their sign and secret –
The stone-work tightly set, the thatching weatherproof,
Double-doors well-hinged; how he had lopped off branches
And with his adze smoothed down the trunk and got it plumb
– The beginnings of a bed, the bedpost – and with his auger
Drilled the frame, inlaying silver, ivory, gold; and then
How he had interwoven thongs of ox-hide, coloured purple –
She believed at last in the master-craftsman, Odysseus,
And tangled like a child in the imaginary branches
Of the tree-house he had built, love poet, carpenter.

GLASS FLOWERS

I

I would bring glass flowers to the broken marriages
Because of their flowering time, the once and for all
Hard petals, cups and saucers from a doll's house,
The imaginary roots that grow into the table.

II

The glass iron cooling in your hand will double as
A darning last, a curve of light beneath the holes:
Let me rock along the seams with it before your
Breath condenses on heels and elbows made of glass.

AUBADE

after Nuala ní Dhomhnaill

It's all the same to morning what it dawns on –
On the bickering of jackdaws in leafy trees;
On that dandy from the wetlands, the green mallard's
Stylish glissando among reeds; on the moorhen
Whose white petticoat flickers around the boghole;
On the oystercatcher on tiptoe at low tide.

It's all the same to the sun what it rises on –
On the windows in houses in Georgian squares;
On bees swarming to blitz suburban gardens;
On young couples yawning in unison before
They do it again; on dew like sweat or tears
On lilies and roses; on your bare shoulders.

But it isn't all the same to us that night-time
Runs out; that we must make do with today's
Happenings, and stoop and somehow glue together
The silly little shards of our lives, so that
Our children can drink water from broken bowls,
Not from cupped hands. It isn't the same at all.

THE FIREPLACE

In the fireplace a pyramid of stones, soul-stones
Remembering the molten core, the Milky Way:
Balanced on top an eggshell full of rainwater
About to boil, if our bodies can get close enough.

THE HIP-BATH

My body has felt like a coalminer's black body
Folded into the hip-bath, a blink of white eyes
And then darkness, warm water coloured by darkness
And the hands that trickle down my dusty spine.

COUCHETTE

With my wife, son, daughter in layers up the walls
This room on wheels has become the family vault.
They have fallen asleep, dreams stopping and starting
As my long coffin wobbles on the top couchette.
Shunted down a siding, we shall wait for centuries
Before hurtling to places we have never seen.
No more than a blink of light, a tinkle of bangles,
The old woman who joins us at Turin will leave
Crusts and a plastic bottle of mineral water.
Soon her space will be taken by a younger lady
We met four thousand years ago in Fiesole,
Her face still to be uncovered, and at her feet
A pet cat who has also been wrapped in bandages.

THE MAN OF TWO SORROWS

Since the day after he was conceived his father
Was killed, he will become The Man of Two Sorrows
Whose mother is wading into the river to delay
His birth, squatting all night on a stepping stone
That flattens his head, headstone pressing fontanel,
Waters breaking under water that nearly drowns him,
Until the morning when he is born and she dies
And the drops of first milk vanish in the river.

CATHEDRAL

I

Between the bells and prayers a flower-seller calls
Prices and flower-names the dome translates to echoes,
As though a pigeon had flapped in from the piazza
And perched on the chalice and sipped the sacrament.

II

Because it was dragged on a cart to the cathedral
By untamed calves, the wooden body has emerged
From candle-smoke and incense and, dressed up as God,
Moves through the market to locate those animals.

III

The puppy supposed to suggest a faithful wife
Has nearly nipped her toes for centuries, and begs
To be taken for a walk outside this building
Where stones eat flesh and moonlight eats the stones.

FONT

for Manus Carson

I

On its little island in the middle of the font
A lamb looks over its shoulder at the furore
Of what appear to be dolphins and porpoises
Leaping out of the holy water, but the details
Have been erased by ripples from priests' fingers
Moving like moorhens or geese or swans landing.

II

A pagan and one of those awkward Protestants
I still can imagine beneath the rose-window
A font for you and for my own son and daughters.
Prose is a river of words washing your name now
And poetry a fountain of vowels and consonants.
On your forehead all waters are holy waters.

IL VOLTO SANTO

We've put a necklace on the naked wood, a crown,
A tunic embroidered with gold, expensive clothes.

Which one of us will fill a sponge with vinegar,
And hoist it upon hyssop, and give him to drink?

LAERTES

When he found Laertes alone on the tidy terrace, hoeing
Around a vine, disreputable in his gardening duds,
Patched and grubby, leather gaiters protecting his shins
Against brambles, gloves as well, and, to cap it all,
Sure sign of his deep depression, a goatskin duncher,
Odysseus sobbed in the shade of a pear-tree for his father
So old and pathetic that all he wanted then and there
Was to kiss him and hug him and blurt out the whole story,
But the whole story is one catalogue and then another,
So he waited for images from that formal garden,
Evidence of a childhood spent traipsing after his father
And asking for everything he saw, the thirteen pear-trees,
Ten apple-trees, forty fig-trees, the fifty rows of vines
Ripening at different times for a continuous supply,
Until Laertes recognised his son and, weak at the knees,
Dizzy, flung his arms around the neck of great Odysseus
Who drew the old man fainting to his breast and held him there
And cradled like driftwood the bones of his dwindling father.

NORTHERN LIGHTS

When you woke me up and showed me through the window
Curtains of silk, luminous smoke, ghost fires,
A convergence of rays above the Black Mountain,
The northern lights became our own magnetic field –
Your hand on my shoulder, your tobacco-y breath
And the solar wind that ruffled your thinning hair.

ANTICLEIA

If at a rock where the resonant rivers meet, Acheron,
Pyriphlegethon, Cocytus, tributary of the Styx, you dig
A pit, about a cubit each way, from knuckles to elbow,
And sacrifice a ram and a black ewe, bending their heads
Towards the outer darkness, while you face the water,
And so many souls of the anaemic dead come crowding in
That you hold them back with your bayonet from the blood
Only to recognise among the zombies your own mother,
And if, having given her blood to drink and talked about home,
You lunge forward three times to hug her and three times
Like a shadow or idea she vanishes through your arms
And you ask her why she keeps avoiding your touch and weep
Because here is your mother and even here in Hades
You could comfort each other in a shuddering embrace,
Will she explain that the sinews no longer bind her flesh
And bones, that the irresistible fire has demolished these,
That the soul takes flight like a dream and flutters in the sky,
That this is what happens to human beings when they die?

THE BALLOON

You are a child in the dream and not my mother.
I float above your head as in a hot air balloon
That casts no shadow on you looking up at me
And smiling and waving and running without a limp
Across the shallow streams and fields of shiny grass
As though there were neither malformation nor pain.
This is the first time ever I have seen you running.
You are a child in the dream and not my mother
Which may be why I call out from the balloon to you:
'Jump over the hedges, Connie, jump over the trees.'

EURYCLEIA

I

Eurycleia fetched a basin, poured cold water into it,
Added hot water, and got ready to wash his feet.
But Odysseus shifted out of the firelight, afraid
She might notice his scar, the key to his identity,
A wound a boar inflicted years back, a flesh-wound.
His wet-nurse cradled his foot in her hands and touched
The scar, and recognising him she let go of his leg
Which clattered into the basin – water everywhere,
Such pain and happiness, her eyes filling with tears,
Her old voice cracking as she stroked his beard and whispered
'You are my baby boy for sure and I didn't know you
Until I had fondled my master's body all over.'

II

I began like Odysseus by loving the wrong woman
Who has disappeared among the skyscrapers of New York
After wandering for thousands of years from Ithaca.
She alone remembers the coppice, dense and overgrown,
Where in a compost of dead leaves the boar conceals
Its bristling spine and fire-red eyes and white tusks.

ICON

When I told you on the day my mother died
'I am an orphan now', you crouched over me
And protected me with your shoulders and hair.
Your tears fell from the ceiling on to my face.
I could not believe that when you came to die
Your breasts would die too and go underground.
Your nakedness, mirrored in the windowpane,
Made of God our icon and our peeping tom.

X-RAY

I gaze at myself before I was born. A shadow
Against her liver and spine I share her body
With my brother's body, two skulls in a basket,
Two sets of bones that show no abnormalities.
I want her to eat the world, giblets, marrow,
Tripes and offal, fish, birds, fields of grain.
But because it is April nineteen thirty-nine
I should look up to the breasts that will weep for me
And prescribe in the dark a salad of landcress,
Fennel like hair, the sky-blue of borage flowers.

EVA BRAUN

The moon beams like Eva Braun's bare bottom
On rockets aimed at London, then at the sky
Where, in orbit to the dark side, astronauts
Read from *Mein Kampf* to a delighted world.

GEISHA

Though the partition opens at a touch
She makes a pin-hole and watches people
Watching the sky where a heavy bomber
Journeys to her mirror and jar of rouge.

BLITZ

They empty the swimming baths and lay out the dead.
There are children who haven't learned to swim, bundled
With budgerigars and tabbies under the stairs.
Shockwaves are wrinkling the water that isn't there.

TEREZÍN

No room has ever been as silent as the room
Where hundreds of violins are hung in unison.

GHETTO

I

Because you will suffer soon and die, your choices
Are neither right nor wrong: a spoon will feed you,
A flannel keep you clean, a toothbrush bring you back
To your bathroom's view of chimney-pots and gardens.
With so little time for inventory or leavetaking,
You are packing now for the rest of your life
Photographs, medicines, a change of underwear, a book,
A candlestick, a loaf, sardines, needle and thread.
These are your heirlooms, perishables, worldly goods.
What you bring is the same as what you leave behind,
Your last belonging a list of your belongings.

II

As though it were against the law to sleep on pillows
They have filled a cathedral with confiscated feathers:
Silence irrefrangible, no room for angels' wings,
Tons of feathers suffocating cherubim and seraphim.

III

The little girl without a mother behaves like a mother
With her rag doll to whom she explains fear and anguish,
The meagreness of the bread ration, how to make it last,
How to get back to the doll's house and lift up the roof
And, before the flame-throwers and dynamiters destroy it,
How to rescue from their separate rooms love and sorrow,
Masterpieces the size of a postage stamp, small fortunes.

IV

From among the hundreds of thousands I can imagine one
Behind the barbed-wire fences as my train crosses Poland.
I see him for long enough to catch the sprinkle of snowflakes
On his hair and schoolbag, and then I am transported
Away from that world of broken hobby-horses and silent toys.
He turns into a little snowman and refuses to melt.

V

For street-singers in the marketplace, weavers, warp-makers,
Those who suffer in sewing-machine repair shops, excrement-
Removal workers, there are not enough root vegetables,
Beetroots, turnips, swedes, nor for the leather-stitchers
Who are boiling leather so that their children may eat;
Who are turning like a thick slice of potato-bread
This page, which is everything I know about potatoes,
My delivery of Irish Peace, Beauty of Hebron, Home
Guard, Arran Banners, Kerr's Pinks, resistant to eelworm,
Resignation, common scab, terror, frost, potato-blight.

VI

There will be performances in the waiting room, and time
To jump over a skipping rope, and time to adjust
As though for a dancing class the ribbons in your hair.
This string quartet is the most natural thing in the world.

VII

Fingers leave shadows on a violin, harmonics,
A blackbird fluttering between electrified fences.

Lessons were forbidden in that terrible school.
Punishable by death were reading and writing
And arithmetic, so that even the junior infants
Grew old and wise in lofts studying these subjects.
There were drawing lessons, and drawings of kitchens
And farms, farm animals, butterflies, mothers, fathers
Who survived in crayon until in pen and ink
They turned into guards at executions and funerals
Torturing and hanging even these stick figures.
There were drawings of barracks and latrines as well
And the only windows were the windows they drew.

ARGOS

There were other separations, and so many of them
That Argos the dog who waited twenty years for Odysseus
Has gone on waiting, still neglected on the manure-heap
At our front door, flea-ridden, more dead than alive
Who chased wild goats once, and roe-deer; the favourite,
A real thoroughbred, a marvel at picking up the scent,
Who even now is wagging his tail and drooping his ears
And struggling to get nearer to the voice he recognises
And dying in the attempt; until like Odysseus
We weep for Argos the dog, and for all those other dogs,
For the rounding-up of hamsters, the panic of white mice
And the deportation of one canary called Pepiček.

PONIES

I
Carved out of the darkness and far below
In the very last working, a stable
Where the pressure transforms into trees
Pit-props, rosettes into sunflowers,
Into grazing nosebags and the droppings
That smoulder among lumps of coal.

II
Like the fuzzy star her forelock covers,
A yarn about a townland somewhere –
Two fields and no more, in one of them
The convergence of three counties, and her
Standing up to the gaskins in foxgloves,
Agrimony, swaying meadowsweet.

IN MEMORY OF CHARLES DONNELLY

Killed in Spain, 27.2.37, aged 22

I

Minutes before a bullet hits you in the forehead
There is a lull in the machine-gun fire, time to pick
From the dust a bunch of olives, time to squeeze them,
To understand the groans and screams and big abstractions
By saying quietly: 'Even the olives are bleeding'.

II

Buried among the roots of that olive tree, you are
Wood and fruit and the skylight its branches make
Through which to read as they accumulate for ever
The poems you go on not writing in the tree's shadow
As it circles the fallen olives and the olive-stones.

THE CAIRN AT DOOAGHTRY

Children lie under the cairn, unhallowed souls
Whose playground should be the duach and the dunes.
No higher than little children walking on tiptoe
Past SS guards at the selections in Terezín,
The cairn has become a scree, the scree a landslide
And a raised beach the memorial to all of them.

STONE-IN-OXNEY

for George Newson

At a table which seems to take root in the lawn
We breakfast late to a single propeller's drone,
The ghost of a Spitfire over Stone-in-Oxney
Or a Stuka, its turning-circle that cloud-gap
Or wherever you point to show me a bird; its dive
Low as the ceiling-beams in Chapel Cottage.
We bump against pilots who hang out of the sky.
Someone's hand is overshadowing the place-names,
Tracking the migration of wheatears and blackcaps
Who cross the Channel and make their landfall here.
Let him spread his fingers on a broken wing, now
Reed warblers are singing at Wittersham Levels
And at Small Hythe and Peening Quarter nightingales.

THE ICE-CREAM MAN

Rum and raisin, vanilla, butter-scotch, walnut, peach:
You would rhyme off the flavours. That was before
They murdered the ice-cream man on the Lisburn Road
And you bought carnations to lay outside his shop.
I named for you all the wild flowers of the Burren
I had seen in one day: thyme, valerian, loosestrife,
Meadowsweet, tway blade, crowfoot, ling, angelica,
Herb robert, marjoram, cow parsley, sundew, vetch,
Mountain avens, wood sage, ragged robin, stitchwort,
Yarrow, lady's bedstraw, bindweed, bog pimpernel.

TRADE WINDS

I

Through Molly Ward's and Mickey Taylor's Locks,
Through Edenderry, Aghalee and Cranagh
To Lough Neagh and back again went Perseverance
And Speedwell carrying turf, coal and cinders.

II

Was it an Armagh man who loaded the boat
With the names of apples for his girlfriend:
Strawberry Cheeks, Lily Fingers, Angel Bites,
Winter Glories, Black Annetts, Widows' Whelps?

III

For smoking at wakes and breaking on graves
Carrick men christened clay pipes in Pipe Lane
Keel Baltic, Swinyard Cutty, Punch Quelp,
Plain Home Rule, Dutch Straws, Bent Unique.

IV

Among the Portavogie prawn-fishermen
Which will be the ship of death: Trade Winds,
Guiding Starlight, Halcyon, Easter Morn,
Liberty, Faithful Promise, Sparkling Wave?

THE BUTCHERS

When he had made sure there were no survivors in his house
And that all the suitors were dead, heaped in blood and dust
Like fish that fishermen with fine-meshed nets have hauled
Up gasping for salt water, evaporating in the sunshine,
Odysseus, spattered with muck and like a lion dripping blood
From his chest and cheeks after devouring a farmer's bullock,
Ordered the disloyal housemaids to sponge down the armchairs
And tables, while Telemachos, the oxherd and the swineherd
Scraped the floor with shovels, and then between the portico
And the roundhouse stretched a hawser and hanged the women
So none touched the ground with her toes, like long-winged thrushes
Or doves trapped in a mist-net across the thicket where they roost,
Their heads bobbing in a row, their feet twitching but not for long,
And when they had dragged Melanthios's corpse into the haggard
And cut off his nose and ears and cock and balls, a dog's dinner,
Odysseus, seeing the need for whitewash and disinfectant,
Fumigated the house and the outhouses, so that Hermes
Like a clergyman might wave the supernatural baton
With which he resurrects or hypnotises those he chooses,
And waken and round up the suitors' souls, and the housemaids',
Like bats gibbering in the nooks of their mysterious cave
When out of the clusters that dangle from the rocky ceiling
One of them drops and squeaks, so their souls were bat-squeaks
As they flittered after Hermes, their deliverer, who led them
Along the clammy sheughs, then past the oceanic streams
And the white rock, the sun's gatepost in that dreamy region,
Until they came to a bog-meadow full of bog-asphodels
Where the residents are ghosts or images of the dead.

VII

THE GHOST ORCHID
(1995)

for John & Janet Banville

You walked with me among water mint
And bog myrtle when I was tongue-tied:
When I shouted at the ferny cliff
You adopted my echo like a child.

FORM

Trying to tell it all to you and cover everything
Is like awakening from its grassy form the hare:
In that make-shift shelter your hand, then my hand
Mislays the hare and the warmth it leaves behind.

AUTUMN LADY'S TRESSES

How does the solitary swan on Dooaghtry Lake
Who knows all about the otter as a glimmer
Among reeds, as water unravelling, as watery
Corridors into the water, a sudden face,
Receive through the huge silence of sand-dunes
Signals from the otters' rock at Allaran Point
About another otter, the same otter, folding
Sunlight into the combers like brown kelp,
Or the dolphins whose waves within waves propel
You and me along the strand like young lovers,
Or the aftermath of lit thistledown, peacock
Butterflies above marram grass, lady's tresses
That wind into their spirals of white flowers
Cowrie shells for decorating your sandy hair?

WATERCOLOUR

for Jeffrey Morgan

Between a chicken's wishbone on the mantelpiece
And, on the window sill, a dolphin's skull, I sit,
My pullover a continuation of the lazy-beds
You study through the window, my shirt a running
Together of earth-colours, wintry grasses, bracken
Painted with your favourite brush – goose-quill and sable
From a hundred years ago – and with water:
One drop too many and the whole thing disintegrates.
In this humidity your watercolour will never dry.

SITTING FOR EDDIE

in memory of Edward McGuire

I had suggested a spray of beech leaves behind me
Or a frieze of birds – bittern, lapwing, chough –
Or a single carline-thistle representing flowers
Pressed between pages, stuffed birds behind glass, our
Still lives, Eddie's and mine, feathers and petals
That get into the picture like noises-off, long
Distance calls in the small hours, crazed arguments
About the colour of my eyes – his strange mistake –
Jazz to relax me, in an enormous magnifying
Glass our eyes out of all proportion, likenesses
And the trundle of castors under a skylight,
His gambler's eye-shield, the colours of the rainbow,
Me turning into a still life whose eyes are blue.

GRETTA BOWEN'S EMENDATIONS

Eighty when she first created pictures, Gretta Bowen
Postponed the finishing touches, and then in her nineties
Emended her world by painting on the glass that covered
Children's games, fairgrounds, swans on a pond, interiors
Not brush-strokes to erase her studious reflection
But additional leaves and feathers falling on to ice.

AFTER HORACE

We postmodernists can live with that human head
Stuck on a horse's neck, or the plastering of multi-
Coloured feathers over the limbs of assorted animals
(So that what began on top as a gorgeous woman
Tapers off cleverly into the tail of a black fish).

Since our fertile imaginations cannot make head
Or tail of anything, wild things interbreed with tame,
Snakes with birds, lambs with tigers. If a retired sailor
Commissions a picture of the shipwreck he survived,
We give him a cypress-tree because we can draw that.

To relieve the boredom we introduce to the woods
A dolphin, a wild boar to the waves. Ultimate post-
Modernists even in the ceramics department we
May have a vase in mind when we start, or a wine-jug,
But, look, as the wheel goes round, it ends up as a po.

THE MAD POET

When someone's afflicted with the itchy nirls
Or jaundice or religious fundamentalism,
You don't play tig with him: ditto the mad poet,
Head in the air, burping pomes, dootering about:

And if, like a wildfowler gawking at blackbirds,
He cope-carlies into a waterhole or heugh
And gulders 'Hi! dear readers! Help!' – do not
Swing him a life-line: sling him a deafie instead.

How do you know he isn't cowping accident-
ally on purpose (and *likes* it down there) just as
That head-the-ball Empedocles a header took
– In hot pursuit of immortality – into Etna?

It's still not clear what hurts him into verse, whether
He pissed on his father's ashes (in the urn) or
Thrappled his muse: at all events he is horn-daft
Like a bear bending the bars of his limitations.

His mad-dog shite has everyone – the poetry-buffs
And the iggerant – shit-scared: he grabbles you, then
He reads you to death, a leech cleeking your skin
Who won't drop off until he is boke-full of blood.

PERDIX

In the wings of that story about the failure of wings
– Broken wings, wings melting, feathers on water, Icarus –
The garrulous partridge crows happily from a sheugh
And claps its wings, a hitherto unheard-of species,
The latest creation, a grim reminder to Daedalus
– Inventor, failure's father – of his apprentice, a boy
Who had as a twelve-year-old the mental capacity
To look at the backbone of a fish and invent the saw
By cutting teeth in a metal blade; to draw conclusions
And a circle with the first compass, two iron limbs,
Arms, legs tied together, geometry's elbow or knee –

Which proved his downfall, for Daedalus grew so jealous
He pushed the prodigy headlong off the Acropolis
And then fibbed about him slipping; but Pallas Athene
Who supports the ingenious, intercepted his fall,
Dressed him in feathers in mid-air and made him a bird,
Intelligence flashing to wing-tip and claw, his name
Passing on to the bird (it is *perdix* in the Greek) –
The partridge that avoids getting airborne and nesting
In tree-tops or on dizzy ledges; that flapping along
At ground level, laying its eggs under hedges, has lost,
Thanks to the memory of that tumble, its head for heights.

ACCORDING TO PYTHAGORAS

When in good time corpses go off and ooze in the heat
Creepy-crawlies breed in them. Bury your prize bull
(A well-known experiment) – and from the putrid guts
Swarm flower-crazy bees, industrious country-types
Working hard, as did their host, with harvest in mind.
An interred war-horse produces hornets. Remove
A shore-crab's hollow claw, lay it to rest: the result
Is a scorpion charging with its tail bent like a hook.
Worms cosy in cocoons of white thread grow into
Butterflies, souls of the dead. Any farmer knows that.

Germs in mud generate green frogs: legless at first
They soon sprout swimming and jumping equipment.
A she-bear's cub is a lump of meat whose stumpy
Non-legs she licks into shape in her own image.
The honey-bees' larvae hatched in those waxy hexagons
Only get feet and wings later on. That's obvious.
Think of peacocks, eagles, doves, the bird-family
As a whole, all starting inside eggs: hard to believe.
There's a theory that in the grave the backbone rots
Away and the spinal cord turns into a snake.

The fundamental interconnectedness of all things
Is incredible enough, but did you know that
Hyenas change sex? The female mounted by a male
Just minutes before, becomes a male herself. Then
There's the chameleon that feeds off wind and air
And takes the colour of whatever it's standing on.
Air transforms lynxes' urine into stones and hardens
Coral, that softly swaying underwater plant.
I could go on and on with these scientific facts.
If it wasn't so late I'd tell you a whole lot more.

SHE-WOLF

Fingers and toes, a tail wagging,
And there in the middle
Rome like a sore belly-button
Peeps out from the huddle.

She licks Romulus and Remus
The moment they piddle,
Her cold nose tickling the heads
That nod off and nuddle.

HIPPOMANES

Randiest of all, taking in their stride mountains
And rapids for sex, biting your hand off, mares,
Kindled in springtime, gonads ablaze, silhouetted
On a cliff where they turn as one to face the wind,
Snuffle the air and often – not a stallion in sight –
Are impregnated:
                    they have been ridden by the wind
And clatter down rocky scree to the valley floor
And scatter, not to the east and sunrise, but south
Where the wind sheds tears from a sky in mourning
And a slippery liquid oozes from their quims,
Hippomanes no less, collected by jealous step-
Mothers and blended with herbs and mumbo-jumbo.

SHEELA-NA-GIG

She pulls her vulva apart for everyone to look at,
Not just for me, a stonemason deflowering stone.
She behaves thus above the church door at Kilnaboy
Where the orchids have borrowed her cunty petals.
A proper libation would be sperm and rainwater.
Ivy grows over her forehead, wall-rue at her feet.

MR 10½

after Robert Mapplethorpe

When he lays out as on a market stall or altar
His penis and testicles in thanksgiving and for sale,
I find myself considering his first months in the womb
As a wee girl, and I substitute for his two plums
Plum-blossom, for his cucumber a yellowy flower.

ROSEMARY

She stood among the nasturtiums on a rubbish dump
And laid on the ground her handkerchief-full of blackberries
And lifted her skirt and moistened the hem with spittle
And dabbed the purple away from the corners of my mouth.

A FLOWERING

Now that my body grows woman-like I look at men
As two or three women have looked at me, then hide
Among Ovid's lovely casualties – all that blood
Colouring the grass and changing into flowers, purple,
Lily-shaped, wild hyacinth upon whose petals
We doodled our lugubrious initials, they and I,
Blood dosed with honey, tumescent, effervescent
 – Clean bubbles in yellow mud – creating in an hour
My own son's beauty, the truthfulness of my nipples,
Petals that will not last long, that hang on and no more,
Youth and its flower named after the wind, anemone.

SPIDERWOMAN

Arachne starts with Ovid and finishes with me.

Her hair falls out and the ears and nostrils disappear
From her contracting face, her body minuscule, thin
Fingers clinging to her sides by way of legs, the rest
All stomach, from which she manufactures gossamer
And so keeps up her former trade, weaver, spider

Enticing the eight eyes of my imagination
To make love on her lethal doily, to dangle sperm
Like teardrops from an eyelash, massage it into her
While I avoid the spinnerets – navel, vulva, bum –
And the widening smile behind her embroidery.

She wears our babies like brooches on her abdomen.

IVORY & WATER

If as a lonely bachelor who disapproves of women
You carve the perfect specimen out of snow-white ivory
And fall in love with your masterpiece and make love to her
(Or try to) stroking, fondling, whispering, kissing, nervous
In case you bruise ivory like flesh with prodding fingers,
And bring sea-shells, shiny pebbles, song-birds, colourful wild
Flowers, amber-beads, orchids, beach-balls as her presents,
And put real women's clothes, wedding rings, ear-rings, long
Necklaces, a brassière on the statue, then undress her
And lay her in your bed, her head on the feathery pillows
As if to sleep like a girlfriend, your dream may come true
And she warms and softens and you are kissing actual lips
And she blushes as she takes you in, the light of her eyes,
And her veins pulse under your thumb at the end of the dream
When she breaks out in a cold sweat that trickles into pools
And drips from her hair dissolving it and her fingers and toes,
Watering down her wrists, shoulders, rib-cage, breasts until
There is nothing left of her for anyone to hug or hold.

MASSIVE LOVERS

after Katsushika Hokusai

I was the philosopher watching a pair of butterflies
Until massive lovers exposed my peedy and grey hairs –
His cock a gate-post, rain running off the glans, snow-broth
And the shriek of silk, hair-pins along the loney – and I
Became the pearl-diver hugged and sucked by octopuses.

A GIFT OF BOXES

I

Rice grains between my chopsticks remind you of a flower.
I want to wash the hagi petals in my bowl, then balance
Before your lips an offering of crabs' brains on a shiso leaf
Which looks like a nettle from Ireland but does not sting.

II

We are completely out of proportion in the tea-house
Until we arrange around a single earthenware bowl
Ourselves, the one life, one meeting, a ribbon of water
And these makeshift ideograms of wet leaves, green tea.

III

You make a gift of boxes by putting boxes inside
Boxes, each one containing the Japanese air you breathe,
More and more of it in diminishing boxes, smallness
Condensing in the end to two boxes the size of tears.

IV

They have planted stones in the stone garden. If I sit still
The stones will take root in my imagination and grow.
You retire behind the fifteenth stone which I cannot see.
Whatever happens to a stone becomes its life, its flower.

A GRAIN OF RICE

Wrap my poem around your chopsticks to keep them clean.
I hardly know you. I do not want you to die. Our names
Fit on to a grain of rice like Hokusai's two sparrows,
Or else, like the praying mantis and the yellow butterfly,
We are a crowd in the garden where nothing grows but stones.
I do not understand the characters: sunlight through leaves,
An ivy pattern like fingers caressing a bowl, your face
In splinters where a carp kisses the moon, the waterfall
Up which its fins will spiral out of sight and into the sky.
Wrap my poem around your chopsticks to keep them clean.
Does it mean I shall not have taken one kiss for ever?
Your unimaginable breasts become the silkworm's shrine.

A PAIR OF SHOES

Who stole my shoes from the Garden of Ryoan-ji?
Have they come near you in Tokyo or Nagoya
Or Takayama? Fifteen rocks make up the landscape
We borrow, faraway places in gravelly sea.

CHINESE OBJECTS

I

The length of white silk I selected
Immaculate as the crust on snow
Was cut in the shape of happiness,
Round as the moon in starry skies.
In and out of her sleeve it slides
Rustling up its own cool weather.
I worry that when autumn comes
And blows away this heatwave,
She will toss the fan into a box
Half way through our love affair.

II

When the water-gourd that dangles
Light as a single leaf from the tree
Goes clickety-clack in the breeze
So that bed-sounds and love-making
Get into my dream, in my dream
I throw it away, for the world
Is not so big, the gourd so small:
They are objects outside my body
That get in the way of sleep.

WIND-FARMER

The wind-farmer's smallholding reaches as far as the horizon.
Between fields of hailstones and raindrops his frost-flowers grow.

CHINESE WHISPERS

'From the south it's a long way
With wildfowlers lying in wait.
How many geese will make it
Through the mist, no-one can say.'

'Don't shoot the last to migrate
From the south: let them fly north.
If you do shoot, shoot them both,
So they won't have to separate.'

KESTREL

Because an electric pylon was the kestrel's perch
I wanted her to scan the motorway's long acre
And the tarmac and grassy patches at the airport
And undress her prey in the sky and beat the air
Above grasshopper and skylark as the wind-fucker.

OASIS

Because the rain fell over a thousand years ago
The sand-grouse does not bury his head like the skink
That swims in the sand – more an eddy than a ripple –
But mounts his ancient reflection and then with wet
Feathers breastfeeds his chicks and irrigates the zenith.

THE SHIP OF THE WIND

after the Dutch

I

The oars, heavy with seaweed, at rest in humid mists;
The home-made sail folded at the edge of the ocean;
And over their unassuming faces, lamp-light
That after a day's work is the soul of evening.

They are eating. Food spicy with peace and friendship;
The child's sleepy happiness soothing the cabin;
The lentils and the fish and the rose-pink radishes;
The mother's breasts rising and falling as she breathes.

II

The sun and the sea have erupted, sheet-lightning,
Fans of fire and silk;
Along the blue mountains of morning
The wind grazes like a gazelle.

I stroll between fountains of light,
Around watery, radiant piazzas
With a fair-haired woman who is singing
In clear tones to the everlasting ocean

This lighthearted air that beguiles me:

'The ship of the wind lies ready for our journey,
The sun and the moon are snow-white roses,
Morning and night are two blue sailors –
We shall return to Paradise.'

BAUCIS & PHILEMON

for Brian & Denise Ferran

In the Phrygian hills an oak tree grows beside a lime tree
And a low wall encloses them. Not far away lies bogland.
I have seen the spot myself. It should convince you
 – If you need to be convinced – that the power of heaven
Is limitless, that whatever the gods desire gets done.

Where a drowned valley makes a sanctuary for water birds
(Divers, coots), a whole community used to plough – until
Jupiter brought Mercury without his wand or wings.
Disguised as humans, they knocked at a thousand houses
Looking for lodgings. A thousand houses slammed the door.

But one house took them in, a cottage thatched with straw
And reeds from the bog. Baucis and Philemon, a kindly
Old couple, had been married there when they were young
And, growing old together there, found peace of mind
By owning up to their poverty and making light of it.

Pointless to look for masters or servants here because
Wife and husband served and ruled the household equally.
So, when these sky-dwellers appeared at their cottage-home
Stooping under the low door to get in, the old man
Brought them stools to sit on, the old woman cushions.

She raked the warm ashes to one side and fanned into life
Yesterday's embers which she fed with leaves and dry bark,
The breath from her old body puffing them into flames.
She hoked around in the roof-space for twigs and firewood,
Broke them up and poked the kindling under her skillet.

She took the cabbage which Philemon had brought her
From the garden plot, and lopped off the outer leaves. He
Lowered a flitch of smoked bacon from the sooty rafters
And carved a reasonable helping from their precious pork
Which he simmered in bubbling water to make a stew.

They chatted to pass the time for their hungry visitors
And poured into a beechwood bucket dangling from its peg
Warm water so that the immortals might freshen up.
Over a sofa, its feet and frame carved out of willow,
Drooped a mattress lumpy with sedge-grass from the river.

On this they spread a coverlet, and the gods sat down.
The old woman tucked up her skirts and with shaky hands
Placed the table in front of them. Because one leg was short
She improvised a wedge and made the surface level
Before wiping it over with a sprig of water-mint.

She put on the table speckly olives and wild cherries
Pickled in wine, endives, radishes, cottage-cheese and eggs
Gently cooked in cooling ashes, all served on crockery.
Next, she produced the hand-decorated wine-jug
And beechwood cups polished inside with yellow wax.

In no time meat arrived from the fireplace piping hot
And the wine, a rough and ready vintage, went the rounds
Until they cleared the table for a second course – nuts
And figs and wrinkly dates, plums and sweet-smelling apples
In a wicker basket, purple grapes fresh from the vines.

The centrepiece was a honeycomb oozing clear honey,
And, over everything, the circle of convivial faces
And the bustle of hospitality. And then the hosts
Noticed that the wine jug, as soon as it was emptied,
Filled itself up again – an inexhaustible supply.

This looked like a miracle to Philemon and Baucis
Who, waving their hands about as if in prayer or shock,
Apologised for their home-cooking and simple recipes.
They had just one gander, guardian of the smallholding,
Whom they wanted to sacrifice for the divinities.

But he was too nippy for them and flapped out of danger
Into the immortals' arms. 'Don't kill the goose!' they thundered.
'We're gods. Your tightfisted neighbours are about to get
What they deserve. You two are granted immunity.
Abandon your home and climb the mountainside with us.'

Unsteady on their walking-sticks they struggled up the steep
Slope and glancing back, a stone's throw from the top, they saw
The townland flooded, with just their homestead high and dry.
While they stood flabbergasted, crying out for neighbours,
Their cottage (a squeeze for the two of them) became a church.

Stone pillars took the place of the home-made wooden piles,
The thatching glowed so yellow that the roof looked golden,
Filigree transformed the doorway, and marble tiling
Improved the dirt floor. Jupiter spoke like a gentleman:
'Grandpa, if you and your good wife could have one wish . . . ?'

'May we work as vergers in your chapel, and, since our lives
Have been spent together, please may we die together,
The two of us at the one time? I don't want to see
My wife buried or be buried by her.' Their wish came true
And up to the last moment they looked after the chapel.

At the end of their days when they were very old and bowed
And living on their memories, outside the chapel door
Baucis who was leafy too watched Philemon sprouting leaves.
As tree-tops overgrew their smiles they called in unison
'Goodbye, my dear'. Then the bark knitted and hid their lips.

Two trees are grafted together where their two bodies stood.
I add my flowers to bouquets in the branches by saying
'Treat those whom God loves as your local gods – a blackthorn
Or a standing stone. Take care of caretakers and watch
Over the nightwatchman and the nightwatchman's wife.'

WATERLILY

I

As if Venus and Betelgeuse had wings
And instead of mountainside or tree-top

Had found the right place for falling stars
And glided to a standstill on the lake ...

II

after Frederik van Eeden

I love the white waterlily, immaculate,
Unfolding her corolla in daylight.

Rising from the cold sediments of the lake
She has seen the light and then unlocked

Her heart of gold: on the surface at one
With herself, her very own creation.

III

Finding my way by night-lights in the sky
I splash through puddles the size of the moon

To a lake the size of the Milky Way
Which I shall call the waterlily lake.

THE SCISSORS CEREMONY

What they are doing makes their garden feel like a big room.
I spy on them through the hedge, through a hundred keyholes.
He sits in a deckchair. She leans over him from behind
As though he were a little boy, and clips his fingernails
Into the newspaper he balances between his knees. Her
White hair tickles his white hair. Her breath at his ear
Might be correcting his sums, disclosing the facts of life,
Recalling the other warm cheeks that have hesitated there.
He is not demented or lazy or incapacitated. No,
It is just that she enjoys clipping his fingernails
And scattering them like seeds out of a rattly packet.
Are they growing younger as I walk the length of the hedge?
Look! The scissors ceremony is a way of making love!

COUPLET

When I was young I wrote that flowers are very slow flames
And you uncovered your breasts often among my images.

LIZARD

So small its brassy hand,
Lightfingered its fingers,
I saw a brooch that you
Could wear next your skin.

I wanted it to curl
Its detachable tail
Under your collar-bone
As though to drink there,

But the moment I moved
It skittered first of all
Between your breasts and then
Over your shoulder.

BLACKBIRD

On our side of the glass
You laid out the blackbird's
Sleepy eyes, its twiggy
Toes, crisp tail-feathers
And its wings wider than
The light from two windows.

CHENAC

for Maurice Hayes

I

Today nothing happens in Chenac except for me
And you in the old bakery Maurice is rebuilding,
Rafters like branches, altar-wide hearth, cobwebby
Cubby-holes where yeast fizzed, bread cooled: our estate
Sweet blackberries and windfalls beside the marguerites;
Our guardians the spider out of the Book of Proverbs
That takes hold with her hands, and is in kings' palaces,
The centipede that shimmies where the cellar will be.

II

On twin pillars in St Martin's church bunches of grapes
And orioles repeat themselves and reach the starry sky
A child painted above the altar; until the bell
Recalls diminutive single sunflowers sprouting here
And there, outcasts that escaped both sowing and harvest;
On the road to Épargnes where you can see our steeple
The buzzard with nowhere to perch but stubbly furrows
Flapping to his mate, a tangle of straw in his talons.

III

Accompanying us indoors before a rain-storm the lizard
Zig-zags into his cranny, who is exceeding wise
And makes his house in the rocks and therefore in this house.

POSEIDON

Standing behind the god Poseidon I can see
Through his buttocks to the scrotum's omega.

When I helped Grandpa George into the bath
The same view led me to my mother and me.

His skin seemed dusted as if by moths' wings,
The creases behind his knees like a little boy's.

The god drops whatever he was brandishing
– Trident or thunderbolt – into the bathwater.

PHOENIX

I'll hand to you six duck eggs Orla Murphy gave me
In a beechwood bowl Ted O'Driscoll turned, a nest
Jiggling eggs from Baltimore to Belfast, from friends
You haven't met, a double-yolk inside each shell
Laid by a duck that renovates and begets itself
Inside my head as the phoenix, without grass or corn,
On a strict diet of frankincense and cardamoms,
After five centuries builds with talons and clean beak
In the top branches of a quivering palm his nest,
Lining it with cassia, spikes of nard, cinnamon chips
And yellow myrrh, brooding among the spicy smells
His own death and giving birth to an only child
Who grows up to carry through thin air the heavy nest
– His cradle, his father's coffin – to the sun's city,
In front of the sun's doorway putting his bundle down
As I shall put down the eggs Orla Murphy gave me
In a beechwood bowl Ted O'Driscoll turned for her.

THE DRY CLEANERS

Poem Beginning with a Line of Raymond Carver

That time I tagged along with my dad to the dry cleaners
We bumped into Eurycleia whose afternoon-off it was
And bought her tea and watched her smooth the table-
Cloth and make her plate and doily concentric circles, then
Pick up cake-crumbs with a moistened finger, since to us
There was more to her than jugs and basins, hot water
And cold, bed-linen she tested against her cheek after
The rainy trek from clothes-line to airing cupboard. Once
She carried a lamp across the yard in front of me
And saw me to my bedroom and folded my clothes and
Smoothed them and hung them on a peg by my wooden bed
And pulled the door to by its silver handle and drew
Home the bolt with the leather strap and left me alone
Worried but cosy through the night under woolly blankets.
Eurycleia the daughter of Ops the son of Peisenor
Took care of me and haunts our wardrobe as the plastic bags
My clothes come back from the dry cleaners shrouded in.

AKROTIRI

Next to the window-frame made out of air, a door
Where ash surrounds and balances a pitcher
As though by itself labour might be mummified
And history left ajar for the water-carrier.

A BED OF LEAVES

He climbed to the copse, a conspicuous place near water,
And crawled under two bushes sprouting from one stem (olive
And wild olive), a thatch so close neither gale-force winds
Nor sunlight nor cloudbursts could penetrate: it was here
Odysseus snuggled and heaped on his mattress of leaves
An eiderdown of leaves, enough to make a double-bed
In winter, whatever the weather, and smiled to himself
When he saw his bed and stretched out in the middle of it
And let even more of the fallen leaves fall over him:
As when a lonely man on a lonely farm smoors the fire
And hides a turf-sod in the ashes to save an ember,
So was his body in the bed of leaves its own kindling
And sleep settled on him like ashes and closed his eyelids.

SNOW-HOLE

Falling asleep in the snowscape of the big double-bed
I wrap my hand around your hand until they catch fire
And the snow begins to melt and we sink down and down,
The fire and ourselves, how many feet below the morning.
Should our fingers burn out at the bottom of the snow-hole
Smoke will escape up the glass chimney into the bedroom.

THE EEL-TRAP

I lie awake and my mind goes out to the otter
That might be drowning in the eel-trap:

                                        your breathing
Falters as I follow you to the other lake
Below sleep, the brown trout sipping at the stars.

THE KILT

I waken you out of your nightmare as I wakened
My father when he was stabbing a tubby German
Who pleaded and wriggled in the back bedroom.

He had killed him in real life and in real life had killed
Lice by sliding along the pleats a sizzling bayonet
So that his kilt unravelled when he was advancing.

You pick up the stitches and with needle and thread
Accompany him out of the grave and into battle,
Your arms full of material and his nakedness.

BEHIND A CLOUD

I

When my father stumbled over gassy corpses
And challenged the shadow of himself on duck-boards,
A field of turnips had filled with German helmets
And under his feet eyes were looking at the moon.

II

When I heard the storm petrel that walks on tiptoe
Over the waves, pattering the surface, purring
And hiccupping, the moon had gone behind a cloud
And changed the sea into a field full of haycocks.

A PAT OF BUTTER

after Hugo Claus

The doddery English veterans are getting
Fewer, and point out to fewer doddery pals
Hill Sixty, Hill Sixty-one, Poelkapelle.

My dad's ghost rummages for his medals
And joins them for tea after the march-past.
The butter tastes of poppies in these parts.

THE CAMPFIRES

All night crackling campfires boosted their morale
As they dozed in no man's land and the killing fields.
(There are balmy nights – not a breath, constellations
Resplendent in the sky around a dazzling moon –
When a clearance high in the atmosphere unveils
The boundlessness of space, and all the stars are out
Lighting up hilltops, glens, headlands, vantage
Points like Tonakeera and Allaran where the tide
Turns into Killary, where salmon run from the sea,
Where the shepherd smiles on his luminous townland.
That many campfires sparkled in front of Ilium
Between the river and the ships, a thousand fires,
Round each one fifty men relaxing in the firelight.)
Shuffling next to the chariots, munching shiny oats
And barley, their horses waited for the sunrise.

CEASEFIRE

I

Put in mind of his own father and moved to tears
Achilles took him by the hand and pushed the old king
Gently away, but Priam curled up at his feet and
Wept with him until their sadness filled the building.

II

Taking Hector's corpse into his own hands Achilles
Made sure it was washed and, for the old king's sake,
Laid out in uniform, ready for Priam to carry
Wrapped like a present home to Troy at daybreak.

III

When they had eaten together, it pleased them both
To stare at each other's beauty as lovers might,
Achilles built like a god, Priam good-looking still
And full of conversation, who earlier had sighed:

IV

'I get down on my knees and do what must be done
And kiss Achilles' hand, the killer of my son.'

THE HELMET

When shiny Hector reached out for his son, the wean
Squirmed and buried his head between his nurse's breasts
And howled, terrorised by his father, by flashing bronze
And the nightmarish nodding of the horse-hair crest.

His daddy laughed, his mammy laughed, and his daddy
Took off the helmet and laid it on the ground to gleam,
Then kissed the babbie and dandled him in his arms and
Prayed that his son might grow up bloodier than him.

THE PARTING

He: 'Leave it to the big boys, Andromache.'
'Hector, my darling husband, och, och,' she.

POPPIES

I

Some people tried to stop other people wearing poppies
And ripped them from lapels as though uprooting poppies
From Flanders fields, but the others hid inside their poppies
Razor blades and added to their poppies more red poppies.

II

In Royal Avenue they tossed in the air with so much joy
Returning wounded soldiers, their stitches burst for joy.

BUCHENWALD MUSEUM

Among the unforgettable exhibits one
Was an official apology for bias. Outside

Although a snowfall had covered everything
A wreath of poppies was just about visible.

No matter how heavily the snow may come down
We have to allow the snow to wear a poppy.

PARTISANS

He hacks at a snowdrift:
She skims the pine needles
That drop into their soup,
Scattering on the snowcrust
Ideograms of 'peace'
And 'love', suchlike ideals.

THE FISHING PARTY

Because he loves off-duty policemen and their murderers
Christ is still seen walking on the water of Lough Neagh,
Whose fingers created bluebottles, meadow-browns, red
Admirals, painted ladies, fire-flies, and are tying now
Woodcock hackles around hooks, lamb's wool, badger fur

Until about his head swarm artificial flies and their names,
Dark Mackerel, Gravel Bed, Greenwell's Glory, Soldier
Palmer, Coachman, Water Cricket, Orange Grouse, Barm,
Without snagging in his hair or ceasing to circle above
Policemen turned by gunmen into fishermen for ever.

THE SCALES

Thick as the snowflakes on a wintry day when God
Comes down as snow and shows mankind his arsenal,
Putting the winds to sleep, blanketing in snowdrifts
Hill-tops, rocky promontories, pasture, turning
Jetties and beaches white, melting for breakers only –
So flew the stones, a snowstorm of stones, and then
A thunderstorm, shields crunching against shields,
Spears splintering, death-rattles, battle cries, dead-
Lock all morning, until God the Father at noon
Adjusted his golden scales, and in them weighed
Death sentences, holding the beam up by the middle
To see whose destiny would wobble heavenwards,
Whose come to rest on life-supporting earth, and whose
Faces, when God thundered, would go white as snow.

PHEMIOS & MEDON

Still looking for a scoot-hole, Phemios the poet
In swithers, fiddling with his harp, jukes to the hatch,
Lays the bruckle yoke between porringer and armchair,
Makes a ram-stam for Odysseus, grammels his knees,
Then bannies and bams wi this highfalutin blether:
'I ask for pity and respect. How could you condemn
A poet who writes for his people and Parnassus,
Autodidact, his repertoire god-given? I beg you
Not to be precipitate and cut off my head. Spare me
And I'll immortalise you in an ode. Telemachos
Your own dear son will vouch that I was no party-hack
At the suitors' dinner-parties. Overwhelmed and out-
Numbered, I gave poetry readings against my will.'
I gulder to me da: 'Dinnae gut him wi yer gully,
He's only a harmless crayter. And how's about Medon
The toast-master whose ashy-pet I was? Did ye ding him
When the oxherd and the swineherd stormed the steading?'
Thon oul gabble-blooter's a canny huer and hears me
From his fox's-slumber in cow-hides under a chair –
Out he spalters, flaffing his hands, blirting to my knees:
'Here I am, dear boy! Put in a word for me before
Your hot-blooded pater slaughters me as one of them –
The suitors I mean, bread-snappers, belly-bachelors.'
Long-headed Odysseus smiles at him and says: 'Wheesht!
You may thank Telemachos for this chance to wise up
And pass on the message of oul dacency. Go out
And sit in the haggard away from this massacre,
You and the well-spoken poet, while I redd the house.'
They hook it and hunker fornenst the altar of Zeus,
Afeard and skelly-eyed, keeking everywhere for death.

HOMER'S OCTOPUS

The poet may be dead and gone, but her/his
Poetry is like Homer's octopus
Yanked out of its hidey-hole, suckers
Full of tiny stones, except that the stones
Are precious stones or semi-precious stones.

CAVAFY'S DESIRES

Like corpses that the undertaker makes beautiful
And shuts, with tears, inside a costly mausoleum
– Roses at the forehead, jasmine at the feet – so
Desires look, after they have passed away
Unconsummated, without one night of passion
Or a morning when the moon stays in the sky.

SORESCU'S CIRCLES

With the three parts of water in my bones and tissues
Coloured blue; two eyes like sea-stars; my forehead
(The driest part) wrinkly, a carbon-copy of the earth's
Crust; my soul at sea making waves: have I the sense
To describe every day two circles – the merry-go-
Round around the sun and the roundabout of death?

THE PLEIADES

The moment I heard that Oisín Ferran had died in a fire
In his flat in Charlemont Street in Dublin, my mind became
The mind of the old woman who for ninety years had lived
In the middle of the Isle of Man and had never seen
The sea – and I helped him drag the smouldering mattress
Past the wash-basin and down the street and down the roads
That lead to the sea and my very first sight of the sea
And the sea put out the fire and washed his hands and face.

But when I knew that he was dead I found this memory
For Oisín of stars clustered on Inishbofin or Inishturk,
A farmstead out in the Atlantic, its kitchen door
Ajar while somebody turns on lights in the outhouses,
As though the sounds of pumps and buckets, boots and bolts
And safe animals – as though these sounds were visible
And had reached us from millions of miles away to sparkle
Like the Pleiades that rise out of the sea and set there.

THE RULES OF BASEBALL

How long have we been hanging above the lights of O'Hare?
I reach beyond the wing and Chicago's skyline to Frank
And Mary's lopsided, laid-back, rickety, wooden home
Where we shall talk about poetry and the rules of baseball.
How many tons do we weigh in the cross-winds? Darkened
Seven-four-sevens are queueing up around the moon.

HEADSTONE

I

The headstone for my parents' grave in Drumbo churchyard
I have imagined only: a triangular slab from the spiral
Staircase in the round tower that nearly overshadows them,
A stumpy ruin beside which I have seen myself standing
And following everyone's forefinger up into the sky.

II

Because he had survived in a coracle made out of feathers
I want to ask him about the lock-keeper's house at Newforge
Where a hole grows in the water, and about the towpath
That follows the Styx as far as the Minnowburn Beeches
And the end of his dream, and about the oars like wings.

III

As though her ashes had been its cargo when the ice-boat
Was rocked at dawn like a cradle and hauled from Shaw's
Bridge past Drumbo and Drumbeg, all the way to Aghalee,
I can hear in the frosty air above Acheron ice cracking
And the clatter of horses' hooves on the slippery towpath.

IV

The wreck at Thallabaun whose timbers whistle in the wind
The tunes of shipwright, sawyer, cabinet-maker – adze
And axe and chisel following the grain – is my blue-print
For the ship of death, wood as hard as stone that keeps
Coming ashore with its cargo of sand and sandy water.

SUN & MOON

Could water take the weight of your illness ever,
Jonathan, in this story, say, about sun and moon
Who build a house with a garden big enough
For water to come and visit, but when water comes
With turtles and dolphins and fish, the garden
Overflows and then the house, floor by floor, until
Sun and moon climb out on to the roof to keep dry
And, finally, into the sky where they now live
And keep an eye on you in their underwater
House swimming through the doors and up the stairs?

BIRDSONG

'Where am I?' Consulting the *Modern School Atlas*
You underline Dalkey in Ireland, in Scotland Barrhead.
'What day is it?' Outside the home, house-sparrows
With precision tweetle and wheep under the eaves.

Although you forget their names, you hear the birds
In your own accent, the dawn chitter, evening chirl,
The woodpigeon's rooketty-coo and curdoo. 'Who
Am I? Where am I?' is what a bird might sing.

ICICLE

Though the caddis-fly does something similar with hailstones
Knitting them into a waistcoat for her shivering larva,
The ants carry snowflakes inside their nest to make an icicle
Which will satisfy the huge queen and her ignorant grubs
And prove that the melting snowman was somebody's child.

THE GHOST ORCHID

Added to its few remaining sites will be the stanza
I compose about leaves like flakes of skin, a colour
Dithering between pink and yellow, and then the root
That grows like coral among shadows and leaf-litter.
Just touching the petals bruises them into darkness.

THE WHITE GARDEN

So white are the white flowers in the white garden that I
Disappear in no time at all among lace and veils.
For whom do I scribble the few words that come to me
From beyond the arch of white roses as from nowhere,
My memorandum to posterity? Listen. 'The saw
Is under the garden bench and the gate is unlatched.'

SNOW BUNTING

for Sarah

At Allaran, the otters' rock, between the breakers'
Uninterrupted rummaging and – from the duach –
Larksong, I mistake your voice for your mother's voice
Deciphering otter prints long before you were born

As though you were conceived in a hayfield so small
Stone walls surrounded a single stook, and the snow
Bunting's putative tinkle from beyond the ridge
Sounded even closer than the spindrift's whispering.

CHINESE OCCASIONS

I

Snow piles up against the sunny window.
I burn my joss-sticks (a religious notion).
A blue tit tweetles from the patio.
The breeze sets a snowy twig in motion.

II

I am inspired by wind off the Lagan.
I tipple in the Black Mountain's shadow.
I fall into the flowerbed (drink taken),
Soil and sky my eiderdown and pillow.

III

They sip their whiskies on the patio.
Listen to them and what they listen to.
I close the door and open the window.
My friends grow feathers from top to toe.

IV

At the heart of the blue wisteria
A blackbird practises its aria.

RIVER & FOUNTAIN

I

I am walking backwards into the future like a Greek.
I have nothing to say. There is nothing I would describe.
It was always thus: as if snow has fallen on Front
Square, and, feeling the downy silence of the snowflakes
That cover cobbles and each other, white erasing white,
I read shadow and snow-drift under the Campanile.

II

'It fits on to the back of a postage stamp,' Robert said
As he scribbled out in tiny symbols the equation,
His silhouette a frost-flower on the window of my last
Year, his page the sky between chimney-stacks, his head
And my head at the city's centre aching for giddy
Limits, mathematics, poetry, squeaky nibs at all hours.

III

Top of the staircase, Number Sixteen in Botany Bay,
Slum-dwellers, we survived gas-rings that popped, slop-
Buckets in the bedrooms, changeable 'wives', and toasted
Doughy doorsteps, Freshmen turning into Sophisters
In front of the higgledy flames: our still-life, crusts
And buttery books, the half-empty marmalade jar.

IV

My Dansette record player bottled up like genies
Sibelius, Shostakovich, Bruckner, dusty sleeves
Accumulating next to Liddel and Scott's *Greek-English
Lexicon* voices the fluffy needle set almost free.
I was the culture vulture from Ulster, Vincent's joke
Who heard *The Rite of Spring* and contemplated suicide.

V

Adam was first to read the maroon-covered notebooks
I filled with innocent outpourings, Adam the scholar
Whose stammer could stop him christening this and that,
Whose Eden was annotation and vocabulary lists
In a precise classicist's hand, the love of words as words.
My first and best review was Adam's 'I like these – I – I – '

VI

'College poet? Village idiot you mean!' (Vincent again).
In neither profession could I settle comfortably
Once Derek arrived reciting Rimbaud, giving names
To the constellations over the Examination Hall.
'Are you Longley? Can I borrow your typewriter? Soon?'
His was the first snow party I attended. I felt the cold.

VII

We were from the North, hitch-hikers on the Newry Road,
Faces that vanished from a hundred driving-mirrors
Down that warren of reflections – O'Neill's Bar, Nesbitt's –
And through Front Gate to Connemara and Inishere,
The raw experience of market towns and clachans, then
Back to Rooms, village of minds, poetry's townland.

VIII

Though College Square in Belfast and the Linen Hall
Had been our patch, nobody mentioned William Drennan.
In Dublin what dreams of liberty, the Index, the Ban:
Etonians on Commons cut our accents with a knife.
When Brendan from Ballylongford defied the Bishop, we
Flapped our wings together and were melted in the sun.

IX

A bath-house lotus-eater – fags, sodden *Irish Times* –
I tagged along with the Fabians, to embarrass Church
And State our grand design. Would-be class-warriors
We raised, for a moment, the Red Flag at the Rubrics,
Then joined the Civil Service and talked of Civil Rights.
Was Trinity a Trojan Horse? Were we Greeks at all?

X

'The Golden Mean is a tension, Ladies, Gentlemen,
And not a dead level': the Homeric head of Stanford
Who would nearly sing the first lines of the *Odyssey*.
That year I should have failed, but, teaching the *Poetics*,
He asked us for definitions, and accepted mine:
'Sir, if prose is a river, then poetry's a fountain.'

XI

Someone has skipped the seminar. Imagine his face,
The children's faces, my wife's: she sat beside me then
And they were waiting to be born, ghosts from a future
Without Tom: he fell in love just once and died of it.
Oh, to have turned away from everything to one face,
Eros and Thanatos your gods, icicle and dew.

XII

Walking forwards into the past with more of an idea
I want to say to my friends of thirty years ago
And to daughters and a son that Belfast is our home,
Prose a river still – the Liffey, the Lagan – and poetry
A fountain that plays in an imaginary Front Square.
When snow falls it is feathers from the wings of Icarus.

THE OAR

I am meant to wander inland with a well-balanced oar
Until I meet people who know nothing about the sea
– Salty food, prows painted purple, oars that are ships'
Wings – and somebody mistakes the oar on my shoulder
For a winnowing fan:
                            the signal to plant it in the ground
And start saying my prayers, to go on saying my prayers
Once I'm home, weary but well looked after in old age
By my family and friends and other happy islanders,
And death will come to me, a gentle sea-breeze, no more than
An exhalation, the waft from a winnowing fan or oar.

DUACH

I can be seen wherever I am standing, at my feet
Silverweed, five yellow petals surrounded by sand,
A sheep-path leading me on through a haze of hawkbit
To the burial mound that dwindles in my absence.

SANDPIPER

What does the sandpiper know of the river changing course,
The dry bed for her eggs that once was the otter's pool,
The heron's pool and the dragonflies', our pool as well
Where we made out of shoulders and shins our cataract?

OUT THERE

Do they ever meet out there,
The dolphins I counted,
The otter I wait for?
I should have spent my life
Listening to the waves.

VIII

THE WEATHER IN JAPAN
(2000)

for Ronald Ewart

In my ideal village the houses lie scattered
Over miles and are called a townland, while in yours
Neighbours live above and below, and a nightcap
Means climbing up steps in the direction of the stars.

Latches click softly in the trees.
James Wright

WATER-BURN

We should have been galloping on horses, their hoofprints
Splashes of light, divots kicked out of the darkness,
Or hauling up lobster pots in a wake of sparks. Where
Were the otters and seals? Were the dolphins on fire?
Yes, we should have been doing more with our lives.

THE LAPWING

Carrigskeewaun in May light has unsettled me.
Each butterwort flourishes an undertaker's lamp
For the poisoned swan unfolding on David's pond
Like a paper flower in a saucer. 'Milkwort,'
I mumble to the piss-scattering wind. 'Why me?'
The lapwing replies and falters like a bi-plane
Above her nest. 'Why me?' The lapwing and I
Watch over each other and we speak in tongues.

THE COMBER

A moment before the comber turns into
A breaker – sea-spray, raggedy rainbows –
Water and sunlight contain all the colours
And suspend between Inishbofin and me
The otter, and thus we meet, without my scent
In her nostrils, the uproar of my presence,
My unforgivable shadow on the sand –
Even if this is the only sound I make.

PALE BUTTERWORT

Pale butterwort's smoky blue colours your eyes:
I thought of this when I tried to put together
Your every feature, but a buzzard distracted me
As it quartered the tree-tops and added its skraik
Or screel to the papery purr of the dragonflies'
Love-flight, and with so much happening overhead
I forgot the pale butterwort there on the ground
Spreading its leaves like a starfish and digesting
Insects that squirm on each adhesive tongue and
Feed the terror in your eyes, your smoky blue eyes.

THE EXCAVATOR

An excavator at Carrigskeewaun is digging
Near the duach, between the lakes, no more than
More space for water and waterbirds, a pond
For you and me to look at from the double-bed.
Imagine a kestrel stooping to tipple there.

THE METEORITE

We crossed the fields by moonlight and by moonlight
Counted the whooper swans, each a white silhouette,
A shape from Iceland, and picked out thirty, was it,
Before we were interrupted by the meteorite
And its reflection that among the swans was lit.

THE FLOCK

I am touching your shoulder and pointing out the seals
Head and shoulders above seal-grey water, hand-swimmers
Who look towards us before they fold shimmery cheeks
Into the ripples and disappear. Are they mating,
We wonder. Or suckling their pups. Or just playing.

Touching your shoulder for a second longer takes me
Below the surface, and there I move among the seals
Without frightening them, a shepherd among his sheep
Going over them all and counting his flock by fives
And rescuing one lamb from the seaweedy tangle.

THE SEAL

Will you remember how we watched the minute hand
Move between two cupids, gilded wings underneath
The Wave by Gustave Courbet, so strong a swimmer
He was nicknamed 'the seal' by local fishermen,

Or how in Chardin's *Vase of Flowers* – tuberoses,
Sweetpeas and carnations, his only surviving flower
Piece – the Chinese vase reflects a window and three
Or four petals have just fallen on to the table?

NIGHT-TIME

Without moonlight or starlight we forgot about love
As we joined the blind ewe and the unsteady horses.

A TOUCH

after the Irish

she is the touch of pink
on crab apple blossom
and hawthorn and she melts
frost flowers with her finger

THE WEATHER IN JAPAN

Makes bead curtains of the rain,
Of the mist a paper screen.

A SPRIG OF BAY

in memory of Sean Dunne, 1956-95

I

Stepping among recent windfalls and couch grass
Like wet raffia unravelling and beech seedlings,
I glimpse this rundown orchard's original plan
In the lofty bay tree and the well it canopies,

And drink spring water to your memory and pick
Leaves for the dried beans in your Cork bedsit
As you appear out of those long-haired bearded days
To accept, Sean, cook and poet, a sprig of bay.

II

I wish I could introduce you to this friend of mine
Who is rebuilding a ruined flax mill as a ruin
– If it is a flax mill, or a mill for grinding wheat
(A millstone leans against the wall) – no matter what,

You walk away from the rainy fields into a rainy
Room, windows that let the winds come in, a chimney
That opens up to a square of sky and ivy. Sean,
Wear like a gigantic bangle the cracked millstone.

III

In the abandoned schoolhouse I shelter from the rain
With hundreds of pupils and look beyond boreen
And hollow bog (the 'spother' in these parts) to where
The last turf was stacked for Old Head and the hookers,

And I imagine you, Sean, as in a game of hide
And seek covering, uncovering the eyes of childhood,
Or else, absent because you laboured through the night,
You are the boy who snoozes on the last turf-cart.

THE WELL AT TULLY

for Nicholas Harmon

I

Looking into the well at Tully, the soul of your estate, I
Nearly tell you that 'come home' in Scots can mean 'be born',
That the Incarnation explains itself in wet fields like these.

Lichens inhale the Mayo weather and make the branches
Lacy on trees your mother grew from apple pips, Irish
Peach, russets and bramleys, blushes that seep through skins.

II

This view of the river from a window-seat attracts you
Like a sea trout, though the Bunowen will turn housebreaker
Lifting the rugs, lapping the tables and chairs, calling up

The lone English sergeant in charge of dykes and bridges,
Formal in red coat and stripes, but from the navel down
Buck-naked, immune to assassination or ridicule –

A legend, as one day the strongest man for miles around
(And the townland's only Protestant) will be, who helps you
Manhandle like an Inca handbarrow-loads of boulders

Onto the scraw-fence, as though you were creating the first
Windbreak in history, where I hunker in November rain
And eavesdrop: 'I'm nineteen stone, and two of them is fat!'

III

Reflections of all who have taken a drink of water here
On hands and knees should linger in the well at Tully
And be given their place indoors, out of the wind and rain.

You are right to carry to your kitchen across the fields
Buckets of spring water, ice-cold always and good as new
Thanks to the caretaker frog in that ferny interior.

BURREN PRAYER

Gentians and lady's bedstraw embroider her frock.
Her pockets are full of sloes and juniper berries.

Quaking-grass panicles monitor her heartbeat.
Her reflection blooms like mudwort in a puddle.

Sea lavender and Irish eyebright at Poll Salach,
On Black Head saxifrage and mountain-everlasting.

Our Lady of the Fertile Rocks, protect the Burren.
Protect the Burren, Our Lady of the Fertile Rocks.

THE FACTORY

for Brendan Kennelly

I open a can of peas and I open up
That factory, balancing on tons of pea-vines
And forking them out of the sky into machines,
Millions of peas on a white conveyor belt, sleepy
Eyes, surfacing from a vat sunk into the floor
A gigantic iron shopping-basket full of cans.

The only student-slave able for hard labour,
Kennelly helps me assemble my rusty bed
In a Nissen hut in the middle of vague England,
And create out of cardboard boxes a mattress,
There to collapse, aching, blistery, and waken
At dawn to a blackbird on the corrugated iron,

Kennelly's voice, long before children and wives
Helping me feel at home amid the productive
Cacophony, cans spiralling down from the roof –
Already the tubby, rollicking, broken Christ
Talking too much, drowning me in his hurlygush
Which makes the sound water makes over stones.

IN THE ILIAD

When I was left alone with our first-born
She turned in the small hours her hungry face
To my diddy and tried to suck that button.
Her spittle condenses on my grey hairs.

We wear them like medals for our children
And even in nakedness look overdressed.
In the *Iliad* spears go through them and,
Later, one's ripped from Agamemnon's chest.

DAMIANA

from the Latin

Forget about Damiana, Rome's one and only
Self-appointed hermaphrodite poet/poetess,
Too lily-livered to publish but blasting others,
Especially the girls – Sulpicia, for instance,
Amorous elegist supreme – taunting Tibullus,
Poetry's true lover among cassia and roses,
Jeering at Propertius's desperate intensity,
Taking the piss out of schoolmasterly Macer
For poems about ornithology and snake bites –
Yes, shooting at song birds while plugging himself/
Herself, his/her name derived from the dried leaves
Of *Turnera diffusa* – damiana – a quack
Medicament for spleen, club-footed iambics,
Blocked bowels, and even sexual impotence.

HEARTSEASE

When Helen, destroyer of cities, destroyer of men,
Slipped the lads a Mickey Finn of wine and heartsease,
Unhappiness's cure, a painkiller strong enough
To keep you dry-eyed for a day even if mummy
Or daddy pegs out, or your brother or son's bumped off
On the doorstep in front of you (an Egyptian drug?),
She hadn't a clue that where I hail from – beyond
The north wind, Hyperborean, or nearly – heartsease
Is kiss-me-quick, kiss-me-behind-the-garden-gate,
That in Donegal this pansy gets mixed up with selfheal.

THE PARODY

If dandering three times around the wooden
Horse, groping the carpentry for a knothole and
Imitating the voices of absent wives, Helen
Had impersonated you, sillier than Diomedes
Would I have fallen for the parody, cried out
And turned death and destruction inside out?

THE VISION OF THEOCLYMENUS

What class of a nightmare are you living through,
Poor bastards, your faces, knees shrouded in darkness,
The atmosphere electric with keening – for it all
Ends in tears – the walls bloody, and the crossbeams
Like branches after a cloudburst drippling blood,
The porch full of zombies, likewise the haggard
Where they jostle to go underground, and no
Sun while deadly marsh-gas envelops the globe?

Though it feels to me like midnight here, I'm not,
As you say, peerie-heedit, in need of help –
With my eyes, ears and two feet, with unimpaired
Intelligence I shall make it through those doors
To the real world, and leave hanging over you
Catastrophe, richly deserved, inescapable.

ALL OF THESE PEOPLE

Who was it who suggested that the opposite of war
Is not so much peace as civilisation? He knew
Our assassinated Catholic greengrocer who died
At Christmas in the arms of our Methodist minister,
And our ice-cream man whose continuing requiem
Is the twenty-one flavours children have by heart.
Our cobbler mends shoes for everybody; our butcher
Blends into his best sausages leeks, garlic, honey;
Our cornershop sells everything from bread to kindling.
Who can bring peace to people who are not civilised?
All of these people, alive or dead, are civilised.

AT POLL SALACH

Easter Sunday, 1998

While I was looking for Easter snow on the hills
You showed me, like a concentration of violets
Or a fragment from some future unimagined sky,
A single spring gentian shivering at our feet.

A PRAYER

In our country they are desecrating churches.
May the rain that pours in pour into the font.
Because no snowflake ever falls in the wrong place,
May snow lie on the altar like an altar cloth.

THE EXHIBIT

I see them absentmindedly pat their naked bodies
Where waistcoat and apron pockets would have been.
The grandparents turn back and take an eternity
Rummaging in the tangled pile for their spectacles.

A LINEN HANDKERCHIEF

for Helen Lewis

Northern Bohemia's flax fields and the flax fields
Of Northern Ireland, the linen industry, brought Harry,
Trader in linen handkerchiefs, to Belfast, and then
After Terezín and widowhood and Auschwitz, you,

Odysseus as a girl, your sail a linen handkerchief
On which he embroidered and unpicked hundreds of names
All through the war, but in one corner the flowers
Encircling your initials never came undone.

A BUNCH OF ASPARAGUS

It was against the law for Jews to buy asparagus.
Only Aryan piss was allowed that whiff of compost.
I bring you a bunch held together with elastic bands.
Let us prepare melted butter, shavings of parmesan,
And make a meal out of the mouthwatering fasces.

A POPPY

When millions march into the mincing machine
An image in Homer picks out the individual
Tommy and the doughboy in his doughboy helmet:
'Lolling to one side like a poppy in a garden
Weighed down by its seed capsule and rainwater,
His head drooped under the heavy, crestfallen
Helmet' (an image Virgil steals – *lasso papavera
Collo* – and so do I), and so Gorgythion dies,
And the poppy that sheds its flower-heads in a day
Grows in one summer four hundred more, which means
Two thousand petals overlapping as though to make
A cape for the corn goddess or a soldier's soul.

POETRY

When he was billeted in a ruined house in Arras
And found a hole in the wall beside his bed
And, rummaging inside, his hand rested on *Keats*
By Edward Thomas, did Edmund Blunden unearth
A volume which 'the tall, Shelley-like figure'
Gathering up for the last time his latherbrush,
Razor, towel, comb, cardigan, cap comforter,
Water bottle, socks, gas mask, great coat, rifle
And bayonet, hurrying out of the same building
To join his men and march into battle, left
Behind him like a gift, the author's own copy?
When Thomas Hardy died his widow gave Blunden
As a memento of many visits to Max Gate
His treasured copy of Edward Thomas's *Poems*.

THE WAR GRAVES

The exhausted cathedral reaches nowhere near the sky
As though behind its buttresses wounded angels
Snooze in a halfway house of gargoyles, rainwater
By the mouthful, broken wings among pigeons' wings.

There will be no end to clearing up after the war
And only an imaginary harvest-home where once
The Germans drilled holes for dynamite, for fieldmice
To smuggle seeds and sow them inside these columns.

The headstones wipe out the horizon like a blizzard
And we can see no farther than the day they died,
As though all of them died together on the same day
And the war was that single momentous explosion.

Mothers and widows pruned these roses yesterday,
It seems, planted sweet william and mowed the lawn
After consultations with the dead, heads meeting
Over this year's seed catalogues and packets of seeds.

Around the shell holes not one poppy has appeared,
No symbolic flora, only the tiny whitish flowers
No one remembers the names of in time, brookweed
And fairy flax, say, lamb's lettuce and penny-cress.

In mine craters so vast they are called after cities
Violets thrive, as though strewn by each cataclysm
To sweeten the atmosphere and conceal death's smell
With a perfume that vanishes as soon as it is found.

At the Canadian front line permanent sandbags
And duckboards admit us to the underworld, and then
With the beavers we surface for long enough to hear
The huge lamentations of the wounded caribou.

Old pals in the visitors' book at Railway Hollow
Have scribbled 'The severest spot. The lads did well'
'We came to remember', and the woodpigeons too
Call from the wood and all the way from Accrington.

I don't know how Rifleman Parfitt, Corporal Vance,
Private Costello of the Duke of Wellingtons,
Driver Chapman, Topping, Atkinson, Duckworth,
Dorrell, Wood come to be written in my diary.

For as high as we can reach we touch-read the names
Of the disappeared, and shut our eyes and listen to
Finches' chitters and a blackbird's apprehensive cry
Accompanying Charles Sorley's monumental sonnet.

We describe the comet at Edward Thomas's grave
And, because he was a fisherman, that headlong
Motionless deflection looks like a fisherman's fly,
Two or three white after-feathers overlapping.

Geese on sentry duty, lambs, a clattering freight train
And a village graveyard encompass Wilfred Owen's
Allotment, and there we pick from a nettle bed
One celandine each, the flower that outwits winter.

THE MOUSTACHE

The moustache Edward Thomas grew to cover up
His aesthete's features, the short-back-and-sides hair-do
That moved him to the centre of modern times, recall
My father, aged twenty, in command of a company
Who, because most of them shaved only once a week
And some not at all, were known as Longley's Babies.

THE CHOUGHS

As they ride the air currents at Six Noggins,
Rolling and soaring above the cliff face
And spreading their wing tips out like fingers,
The choughs' red claws recall my father

Telling me how the raw recruits would clutch
Their 'courting tackle' under heavy fire:
Choughs at play are the souls of young soldiers
Lifting their testicles into the sky.

ANNIVERSARY

12 January, 1996

He would have been a hundred today, my father,
So I write to him in the trenches and describe
How he lifts with tongs from the brazier an ember
And in its glow reads my words and sets them aside.

THE BULLET HOLE

Imagine Uncle Matt, head full of Henryson
And Fergusson and fear of death and excitement,
After coming through the North African Campaign
Sweating it out up the steep road to Fiesole
Past the cathedral and the Roman amphitheatre,
The tombs and the temple, at the top of the hill
Turning into this road and approaching this house
And this garden where we sit with an old friend
Between peach and pomegranate trees, a pergola
And all that is left of an Etruscan wall, then
Opening fire, nervously, once, because he thinks
There are Germans in the kitchen, and leaving
In the chestnut crossbeam a hole, a stray bullet
That has taken half a century to find its mark.

THE CENOTAPH

They couldn't wait to remember and improvised
A cenotaph of snow and a snowman soldier,
Inscribing 'Lest We Forget' with handfuls of stones.

DEATH OF A HORSE

after Keith Douglas

Its expression resigned, humble even, as if it knows
And doesn't mind when the man draws the first diagonal
In white across its forehead, from ear to eyeball, then
The second, death's chalky intersection, the crossroads

Where, moments before the legs stiffen and relax and
The knees give way and like water from a burst drain
The blood comes jetting out, black almost, warm and thick,
The horse goes on standing still, just staring ahead.

THE HORSES

For all of the horses butchered on the battlefield,
Shell-shocked, tripping up over their own intestines,
Drowning in the mud, the best war memorial
Is in Homer: two horses that refuse to budge
Despite threats and sweet-talk and the whistling whip,
Immovable as a tombstone, their heads drooping
In front of the streamlined motionless chariot,
Hot tears spilling from their eyelids onto the ground
Because they are still in mourning for Patroclus
Their charioteer, their shiny manes bedraggled
Under the yoke pads on either side of the yoke.

OCEAN

Homage to James 'Mick' Magennis VC

At the performance of Merce Cunningham's *Ocean*
In the Waterfront Hall the coral-coloured dancers
Drenched my head with silence and whale messages
And made me feel like a frogman on dry land.

There was room for only one midget submarine
In the roof space where my mind had floated, and where
Swimming from the Falls Road Baths to Singapore
Mick Magennis emerged in his frogman's suit,

Oxygen leaking in telltale bubbles up to heaven,
His expression unfathomable behind the visor
But his modest thumbs-up confirming that, yes,
He had stuck limpet mines on the cruiser *Takao*.

Alongside dog-paddling, ballet-dancing polar bears,
Penguins like torpedoes, dolphins in twos and threes,
Sea otters, seals, Mick was formation-swimming and
At home in the ocean's cupola above my head.

THE SEWING MACHINE

George Fleming is making out of sailors' collars
A quilt that will cover the sea bed and the graves
Of submariners in their submarines. Listen
As his sewing machine cruises among the flotsam
And picks up hundreds of waterlogged cap tallies:
Stonehenge sunk off the Nicobar Islands, *Spearfish*
And *Salmon* off Norway, *Unbeaten* and *Snapper*
In the Bay of Biscay, in the Gulf of Taranto
Tempest and *Odin* – torpedoes, depth charges,
Mines – *Pandora, Thunderbolt, Narwhal, Urge*
And *Porpoise,* the last submarine sunk in the war.

SWEETIE PAPERS

When sweeties came back to Mrs Parker's shop we
Drooled over the look of them and smoothed out at home
Tinfoil and cellophane, a little bit like Pierre
Bonnard's collection of sweetie papers, his 'sparkles'
Pinned to the wall, light-conductors for the late
Self-portraits as Japanese soldier or collaborator
Punched and kicked in the face until his eyes close
Or death camp survivor, the skin across his chest
Transparent as cigarette paper, and we gazed
Through the squares as through a stained glass window
And almost understood why the unremembered
People sheltering inside the bombed cathedral
Would linger in the changing light, then disappear
Before the end of the war and the end of rationing.

THE EVENING STAR

in memory of Catherine Mercer, 1994-96

The day we buried your two years and two months
So many crocuses and snowdrops came out for you
I tried to isolate from those galaxies one flower:
A snowdrop appeared in the sky at dayligone,

The evening star, the star in Sappho's epigram
Which brings back everything that shiny daybreak
Scatters, which brings the sheep and brings the goat
And brings the wean back home to her mammy.

BROKEN DISHES

Sydney our mutual friend is kneeling by your bed
Hour after hour on the carpetless hospital floor.
He repeats the same kind words and they become
An invocation to you and you start to die.

You love your body. So does Sydney. So do I.
Communion is blankets and eiderdown and sheets.
All I can think of is a quilt called *Broken Dishes*
And spreading it out on the floor beneath his knees.

THE SNOW LEOPARD

in memory of Fiona Jackson, 1970-95

I

I couldn't recommend to you the Elysian Fields
At the world's end with fair-haired Rhadamanthus,
Though there, Fiona, you would still be you, your body
Temperature controlled by westerlies off the waves,

No snowfall, according to the old man of the sea,
No cold spells or cloudbursts to help you feel at home,
No wreaths of frost flowers on your bedroom window,
No snowman in the garden as your memorial.

II

Let me add mine to all the bouquets wrapped in tinfoil
And tied to the bollard where your car careered
A mile from Sandymount, a mile from where your cat
Curled in and out of our one and only conversation.

III

The snow leopard that vanishes in a whirlwind of snow
Can be seen stalking on soft paws among the clouds.

AN ELEGY

in memory of George Mackay Brown

After thirty years I remember the rusty scythe
That summarised in the thatch the deserted village,

And the anchor painted silver so that between showers
Between Hoy and Stromness it reflected the sunshine.

Now the anchor catches the light on the ocean floor.
The scythe too is gleaming in some underwater room.

THE DAFFODILS

Your daughter is reading to you over and over again
Wordsworth's 'The Daffodils', her lips at your ear.
She wants you to know what a good girl you have been.
You are so good at joined-up writing the page you
Have filled with your knowledge is completely black.
Your hand presses her hand in response to rhyme words.
She wants you to turn away from the wooden desk
Before you die, and look out of the classroom window
Where all the available space is filled with daffodils.

THE MUSTARD TIN

You are dying and not sleeping soundly because
Your eyes stay open and it doesn't seem to hurt.
We want you to blink and find three of us standing
For a few seconds between you and the darkness.

Your mouth has opened so wide you appear to scream.
We will need something to close your terrible yawn.
I hoke around in my childhood for objects without
Sharp edges and recover the oval mustard tin.

A daughter strokes your forehead and says: 'There. There.'
A daughter holds your hand and says: 'I'm sorry.'
I focus on the mustard tin propping your jaw,
On the total absence of the oval mustard tin.

THE ALTAR CLOTH

in memory of Marie Ewart

I

You poked your knitting needles through the ball of wool
And laid them beside your glasses on an open book.
You gave the fish in your fish soup a German name.
To begin with you seemed small and elderly to me.

Then you expanded and grew young and beautiful,
Your laughter a wild duck's navigational call,
Your argumentativeness Alexandrian, obstreperous
Your liking for big obstreperous dogs with big tails.

Wherever you are I would have in your vicinity
Wild figs ripening along the bumpiest side-road
And, even if an adder dozes near that carpet,
Masses of cyclamens on the path to the waterfall.

II

In the Piazza Vecchia there are only two houses,
Yours and San Rocco's chapel, so diminutive
It fits like a kennel the saint and the faithful dog
That brings him a loaf of bread daily in the story.

The falling star we saw the night before his festival
May have had nothing to do with his birthmark
Shaped like a cross, or the plague sore on his thigh
He keeps lifting the hem of his tunic to show us,

But, for the split second it managed to stay alight,
The meteor was heading for your household and his
Which is furnished with one table, candlesticks
And shell cases from the last war filled with flowers.

Think of San Giorgio's church who takes the dragon on
And leaves hardly any room for the undersized saint
Balancing the altar on his head, custodian,
We agree, of all we love about the Romanesque.

Shouldn't we be sheltering beneath the altar cloth's
Pattern of grapes and vine leaves, for this is our last
Conversation and the crab is nipping your synapses,
Sifting your memory through its claws and frilly lips?

Marie, I only know this in retrospect. Otherwise
I'd have washed your hair and tranquillised your brain
With evening mist that fills the Valle del Serchio and
Lingers at the bottom of the village between the vines.

MAUREEN MURPHY'S WINDOW

Because you've built shelves across the big window, keep-
Sakes and ornaments become part of the snowy garden.

The footprints we and the animals leave in the snow
Borrow the blue from the blue glassware you collect.

I imagine your dead husband moving in and out
Through window and shelves without breaking a thing.

He is the snow poet and he keeps his snow shoes on.

THE LATECOMERS

for Britta Olinder

One week late for Helena Hallqvist's ninetieth birthday,
We see her for the first time in the *gamla kyrka*.
Sitting at right angles to us, she gazes ahead
At the pulpit and the candles the sun doesn't put out.

She looks up at the ceiling built like a hull, at Christ
Straddling a rainbow that fades into the woodwork.
From just in front of her earlobe three dainty wrinkles
Ripple outwards as crinkles at her daughter's ear.

'The kingdom of heaven is like this,' the pastor begins.
We are the latecomers in his sermon, the labourers
Hired at the eleventh hour and paid an equal wage
To those who bore 'the burden and heat of the day'.

We are not too late for her birthday, who have sweated
For only one hour in the vineyard and earned our penny.

BJÖRN OLINDER'S PICTURES

I have learned about dying by looking at two pictures
Björn Olinder needed to look at when he was dying:
A girl whose features are obscured by the fall of her hair
Planting a flower,

               and a seascape: beyond the headland
A glimpse of immaculate sand that awaits our footprints.

THE SHAKER BARN

I would lie down with you here, side by side,
Our own memorials in what amounts to
The Shakers' cathedral, this circular hay barn,
The two of us fieldmice under storeys of hay,

Tons of hay, a column of hay that changes
The ceiling into a gigantic waggon wheel
Or a rose window made entirely of wood
Which we can see through as far as the sky.

THE HUT

If the hut still existed, I would take you there
To contemplate the waterfall at Glenariff
Through three panes of glass the colour of dawn
And noon and sunset, a cobwebby perspective,

A windy, wide-open snug, a shrine to daylight,
Our time together measured by water falling
And the silence beneath the roar, a pebble
That rotates and dwindles in its rumbling hole.

THE DESIGN

Sometimes the quilts were white for weddings, the design
Made up of stitches and the shadows cast by stitches.
And the quilts for funerals? How do you sew the night?

THE YELLOW TEAPOT

When those who had eaten at our table and drunk
From the yellow teapot into the night, betrayed you
And told lies about you, I cried out for a curse
And wrote a curse, then stitched together this spell,
A quilt of quilt names to keep you warm in the dark:

Snake's Trail, Shoo Fly, Flying Bats, Spider Web,
Broken Handle, Tumbling Blocks, Hole in the Barn
Door, Dove at the Window, Doors and Windows,
Grandmother's Flower Garden, Sun Dial, Mariner's
Compass, Delectable Mountains, World without End.

FOUND POEM

after Ann Petry

As it developed, Harriet Tubman,
Conductor on the Underground Railroad
Which was really the long road to the North
And emancipation for runaway slaves,
Thought her quilt pattern as beautiful
As the wild flowers that grew in the wood
And along the edges of the roads. The
Yellow was like the Jerusalem flower,
And the purple suggested motherwort,
And the white pieces were like water
Lily, and the varying shades of green
Represented the leaves of all the plants,
And the eternal green of the pine trees.

THE QUILT

for Peggy O'Brien

I come here in the dark, I shall leave here in the dark –
No time to look around Amherst and your little house,
To talk of your ill father, my daughter's broken – no,
There isn't time – tears in the quilt, patterns repeating.

And yet as antique orphan and girlish granny we
Stitch a square of colour on the darkness, needle-
Work, material and words, Emily's bedroom window
With a bowl of flowers we pick out through the glass.

An iron bedstead you brought over from Tralee fills up
The box-room where I snooze, as though I have become
For these few hours in February your father, your son,

While in your neighbourhood instead of snow the bushes
Wear quilts left out all night to dry, like one enormous
Patchwork spring-cleaned, well-aired, mended by morning.

THE SUNBURST

Her first memory is of light all around her
As she sits among pillows on a patchwork quilt
Made out of uniforms, coat linings, petticoats,
Waistcoats, flannel shirts, ball gowns, by Mother
Or Grandmother, twenty stitches to every inch,
A flawless version of *World without End* or
Cathedral Window or a diamond pattern
That radiates from the smallest grey square
Until the sunburst fades into the calico.

THE LEVEL CROSSING

The ticks her children and the two dogs bring in from the fields
Are all that's wrong with living here, says the young woman
Who sits beside me. And the spring rains. The bus driver
Worries about hitting deer on the road and recites his recipe
For marinading venison. Plenty of oregano and garlic.

The freight train trundles for ages through the centre of town.
On the other side of the track the endlessness of Illinois
Awaits us, and the sky teetering around a solitary tree.
I forget to ask about the cure for ticks. I want to go home.
A deer's leap in the dark. Patience at the level crossing.

LEAVING ATLANTA

I shall miss my students and the animals – chipmunks
Vanishing into the lawn, on their twiggy trampoline
The squirrels, a raccoon activating the alarm lights,
'He who scratches with his hands', the Indians named him,
And no visitors to the verandah more ghostly than
The lugubrious opossum and her child – my students
And the animals combining underground, overhead,
Wherever the mind goes in the small hours, at sunrise.

THE DIAMOND

In the dungy dusk of Jessica Tyrrell's
Pony's stable in Kildalkey, the diamond
On Rusty's forehead concentrates the light
Like a beacon for nesting house martins
Lost in the roof space, an artistic touch,
A splash of birdlime, a blaze in the brain.

THE BRANCH

The artist in my father transformed the diagonal
Crack across the mirror on our bathroom cabinet
Into a branch: that was his way of mending things,
A streak of brown paint, dabs of green, an accident
That sprouted leaves,
                              awakening the child in me
To the funny faces he pulls when he is shaving.
He wears a vest, white buttons at his collarbone.
The two halves of my father's face are joining up.
His soapy nostrils disappear among the leaves.

PAPER BOATS

Homage to Ian Hamilton Finlay

fold paper boats
for the boy Odysseus
and launch them

ship-shape
happy-go-lucky
in the direction of Troy

SCRAP METAL

I

Helen Denerley made this raven out of old iron,
Belly and back the brake shoes from a lorry, nuts
And bolts for legs and feet, the wings ploughshares
('Ridgers', she elaborates, 'for tatties and neeps'),
The eyeballs cogs from a Morris Minor gearbox.

The bird poses on the circular brass tray my mother
(And now I) polished, swipes of creamy Brasso,
Then those actions, melting a frosty window pane,
Clearing leaves from a neglected well, her breath
Meeting her reflection in the ultimate burnish.

The beak I identified first as a harrow tooth
Is the finger from an old-fashioned finger-bar
Mower for dividing and cutting down the grass,
And, as he bends his head to drink, the raven points
To where the surface gives back my mother's features.

II

The head I pat is made out of brake calipers
With engine mountings from a Toyota for ears,
The spine a baler chain, the ruff and muscular neck
Sprockets, plough points, clutch plate, mower blades,

The legs a Morris Minor kingpin or swingle tree.
Snow in Aberdeenshire and Helen's garden. A wolf
At the forest's edge where scrap metal multiplies
Waits on claw-hammer feet for the rest of the pack.

THE RABBIT

for Ciaran Carson

I closed my eyes on a white horse pulling a plough
In Poland, on a haystack built around a pole,
And opened them when the young girl and her lover
Took out of a perforated cardboard shoe-box
A grey rabbit, an agreeable shitty smell,
Turds like a broken rosary, the slow train
Rocking this dainty manger scene, so that I
With a priestly forefinger tried to tickle
The narrow brain-space behind dewdrop eyes
And it bounced from her lap and from her shoulder
Kept mouthing 'prunes and prisms' as if to warn
That even with so little to say for itself
A silly rabbit could pick up like a scent trail
My gynaecological concept of the warren
With its entrances and innermost chamber,
Or the heroic survival in Warsaw's sewers
Of just one bunny saved as a pet or meal,
Or its afterlife as *Hasenpfeffer* with cloves
And bay leaves, onions – enough! – and so
It would make its getaway when next I dozed
Crossing the Oder, somewhere in Silesia
(Silesian lettuce, h'm), never to meet again,
Or so I thought, until in Lodz in the small hours
A fat hilarious prostitute let that rabbit bop
Across her shoulders without tousling her hair-do
And burrow under her chin and nuzzle her ear
As though it were crooning 'The Groves of Blarney'
Or 'She Walked Unaware', then in her cleavage
It crouched as in a ploughed furrow, ears laid flat,
Pretending to be a stone, safe from stoat and fox.

THE FOX

Where the burn separating Carrigskeewaun
From Thallabaun crosses the path to the cottage
And fencing crosses the water, flood water
Has hung among grass clumps and black plastic
A fox who tries to sidestep death, decay
And barbed wire by foxtrotting upside down
Against the camber of the Milky Way.

THE HARE

Through a grille of rushes and yellowing grass
You watch me come and go at Carrigskeewaun,
Until I loom over your form like Mweelrea,

Your draughty lackadaisical basket still warm,
Still warm the earth that was rough and ready
Even when you were born, your blue eyes open.

You juke and disappear behind the cottage,
Then lollop after me to Lucca and join
Elephant, wild boar, dromedary on the façade.

You leave pawprints in marble and your grassy
Boat-shape with its inch of improvised rigging
Sets sail past the cottage and the cathedral.

LEOPARDI'S SONG THRUSH

Have they eaten all the thrushes here in Italy?
In the resonant Valle del Serchio I have heard
Thunder claps, church bells, the melancholy banter
Of gods and party-goers, echoes from mountaintops
And Alessandro's hillside bar, but not one thrush.

Rather than the missel thrush, the stormcock fluting
Through bad weather on its diet of mistletoe,
I mourn five or six sky-coloured eggs, anvil stones
For tenderising snails, repetitious phrases,
Leopardi's thrush, the song thrush in particular.

My lamentation a batsqueak from the balcony,
I stick some thorns onto the poet's beloved broom
And call it gorse (or whin or furze), a prickly
Sanctuary for the song thrush among yellow flowers,
Its underwing flashing yellow as it disappears.

THE MUSICAL BOX

As well as querulous house martins and the bells
That clang out from San Ginese's to waken up
The terracotta tortoise dozing between the tongs
And the wood stove, and distract the bronze herons,
One listening to the ceiling, the other to the floor,

There is so much music in your house, it contracts
In my mind to a musical box with room enough
For the old woman who ran a kindergarten
In this kitchen – simple addition, tonic solfa –
And for the man who kept canaries under the roof.

ETRURIA

Pavese's English poems, an English setter barking –
Too hot and clammy to read, sleep, dander, so
Snap my walking stick in two and lay it out beside
My long bones in an ossuary that tells a story,

The apprentice ivory carver's yarn, for instance,
Who etched those elderly twinkling Chinese pilgrims
On a walnut, shell-crinkles their only obstacle,
Globe-trotters in my palm, the kernel still rattling.

You can find me under the sellotaped map fold
Stuck with dog hairs, and close to a mulberry bush
The women tended, coddling between their breasts
The silkworms' filaments, vulnerable bobbins.

Was it a humming bird or a humming bird moth
Mistook my navel for some chubby convolvulus?
Paolo steps from his *casa* like an astronaut
And stoops with smoky bellows among his bees.

Gin, acacia honey, last year's sloes, crimson
Slipping its gravity like the satellite that swims
In and out of the hanging hornet-traps, then
Jukes between midnight planes and shooting stars.

The trout that dozed in a perfect circle wear
Prison grey in the fridge, bellies sky-coloured
Next to the butter dish's pattern, traveller's joy,
Old man's beard when it seeds, feathery plumes.

The melon Adua leaves me on the windowsill
Gift-wrapped in a paper bag and moonlight,
Ripens in moon-breezes, the pipistrelle's whooshes,
My own breathing and the insomniac aspen's.

A liver concocted out of darkness and wine
Dregs, the vinegar mother sulking in her crock
Haruspicates fever, shrivelled grapes, vipers
On the footpath to a non-existent waterfall.

I escape the amorous mongrel with dewclaws
And vanish where once the privy stood, my kaftan
Snagging on the spiral staircase down to the small
Hours when house and I get into bed together,

My mattress on the floor, crickets, scorpion shapes
In their moonlit square, my space in this cellar
Beneath old rafters and old stones, Etruria,
Nightmare's cesspit, the mosquito-buzz of sleep.

PASCOLI'S PORTRAIT

Dining under your portrait at Ponte di Campia
I need hardly apologise for not knowing
Your poetry, although I hear wingbeats and see
An eye that sees the skylark and the skylark's eye.

Since a poem's little more than a wing and a prayer,
I turn back to my dinner and pretend our souls
Are roosting on the broken lamp beneath the eaves.
Splashes of birdlime on the pavement give us away.

REMEMBERING THE POETS

As a teenage poet I idolised the poets, doddery
Macer trying out his *Ornithogonia* on me,
And the other one about herbal cures for snake bites,
Propertius, my soul mate, love's polysyllabic
Pyrotechnical laureate reciting reams by heart,
Ponticus straining to write The Long Poem, Bassus
(Sorry for dropping names) iambic to a fault,
Horace hypnotising me with songs on the guitar,
Virgil, our homespun internationalist, sighted
At some government reception, and then Albius
Tibullus strolling in the woods a little while
With me before he died, his two slim volumes
An echo from the past, a melodious complaint
That reaches me here, the last of the singing line.

FRAGMENT

after Attila József

Forty years I've been at it, working hard,
A poetic pro, no longer the neophyte.
I'm standing near the metalworker's yard
And can't find the words for this starry night.

THE BLACKTHORN

A bouquet for my fifties, these flowers without leaves
Like easter snow, hailstones clustering at dayligone –
From the difficult thicket a walking stick in bloom, then
Astringency, the blackthorn and its smoky plum.

THE BEECH TREE

Leaning back like a lover against this beech tree's
Two-hundred-year-old pewter trunk, I look up
Through skylights into the leafy cumulus, and join
Everybody who has teetered where these huge roots
Spread far and wide our motionless mossy dance,
As though I'd begun my eclogues with a beech
As Virgil does, the brown envelopes unfolding
Like fans their transparent downy leaves, tassels
And prickly cups, mast, a fall of vermilion
And copper and gold, then room in the branches
For the full moon and her dusty lakes, winter
And the poet who recollects his younger self
And improvises a last line for the georgics
About snoozing under this beech tree's canopy.

BIRDS & FLOWERS

for Fuyuji Tanigawa

My local The Chelsea where I took you for a pint
Has been demolished, which leaves us drinking in the rain,
Two inky smiles on handkerchiefs tied for luck like dolls
Flapping where the window should be, in Ireland or Japan.

A wagtail pauses among maple leaves turning from red
To pink in the picture you enclose with your good news:
'I have been a man of home these years,' you write, 'often
Surprised to know so much passion hidden in myself.'

You who translated for me 'ichigo-ichie' as 'one life,
One meeting' as though each encounter were once-in-a-
Lifetime, have been spending time with your little children:
'But I will go back to the world of letters soon.' Fuyuji,

The world of letters is a treacherous place. We are weak
And unstable. Let us float naked again in volcanic
Pools under the constellations and talk about babies.
The picture you sent to Belfast is called 'Birds & Flowers'.

THE GARDEN

When Nausicaa described to Odysseus how her mother
Would sit at the hearth as a rule and embroider by firelight
A delightful picture with yarn the colour of sea-purple,
Her chair against a pillar, the maidservants seated behind
And her father up on his throne sipping wine like a god,
Was she proposing what he would later find out for himself
In the spacious garden, four acres surrounded by fences,
Where the trees grow tall and leafy, pear and pomegranate,
Apple with its shiny crop, sweet fig and opulent olive,
Fruit that never runs out, summer or winter, all year
The breathy west wind germinating and ripening apple
After apple, pear after pear, grape cluster on grape cluster,
Fig upon fig; in a sun-trap the sun sun-drying grapes
While others are picked for eating or the wine press, nearby
Green bunches casting their blossom or darkening a little,
And the well-ordered vegetable plots, herbs, perennials,
The whole garden irrigated by one spring, another
Gushing under the haggard gate to supply the big house?

THE WATERFALL

If you were to read my poems, all of them, I mean,
My life's work, at the one sitting, in the one place,
Let it be here by this half-hearted waterfall
That allows each pebbly basin its separate say,
Damp stones and syllables, then, as it grows dark
And you go home past overgrown vineyards and
Chestnut trees, suppliers once of crossbeams, moon-
Shaped nuts, flour, and crackly stuffing for mattresses,
Leave them here, on the page, in your mind's eye, lit
Like the fireflies at the waterfall, a wall of stars.

INVOCATION

Begin the invocation: rice cakes, say, buckwheat
Flowers or temple bells, bamboo, a caged cricket
Cheeping for the girl who plants the last rice seed.
I have a good idea of what's going on outside.

IX

SNOW WATER

(2004)

for David Cabot

Above Caher Island the same cloud hangs
As yesterday, shaped like a sea-horse, the sky
A pink ceiling, the sea a damselfly blue.

The hare sees this as she circles your cottage
Which is just another erratic boulder,
So does the otter stepping out of the waves.

... the sparks of his father curved
into the west of the lake ...
　　　　　　　Medbh McGuckian

SNOW WATER

A fastidious brewer of tea, a tea
Connoisseur as well as a poet,
I modestly request on my sixtieth
Birthday a gift of snow water.

Tea steam and ink stains. Single-
Mindedly I scald my teapot and
Measure out some Silver Needles Tea,
Enough for a second steeping.

Other favourites include Clear
Distance and Eyebrows of Longevity
Or, from precarious mountain peaks,
Cloud Mist Tea (quite delectable)

Which competent monkeys harvest
Filling their baskets with choice leaves
And bringing them down to where I wait
With my crock of snow water.

MOON CAKES

The wee transcendental mountain cottage
is where I continue painting almond
and plum blossom into extreme old age
(i.e. late winter, a covering of snow,
the full moon's unattainability
brightening my dilapidated studio);
is where I overdose on jasmine tea and
moon cakes (a complicated recipe).

FLIGHT FEATHERS

I

It was I who placed the nest-box under our bedroom
Window and inspired the nuptial flight, flight feathers
Shivering like a moth close to where we snuggle.
This is the blue tits' wheezy epithalamion.

II

I took this down from the electricity line
Where a redwing was recommending *sleep sleep.*
At the lopsided gatepost my only merlin
Was going on about golden plover, wisps of snipe.

III

Will you remember that rainbow in Leitrim low
As the fields, an extra hedge no one had cleared
From the poor land, a long acre no one had drained,
Cover for all of the birds that have disappeared?

IV

The tide-digested burial mound has almost gone.
A peregrine is stooping high above my breastbone.

ARRIVAL

It is as though David had whitewashed the cottage
And the gateposts in the distance for this moment,
The whooper swans' arrival, with you wide awake
In your white nightdress at the erratic boulder
Counting through binoculars. Oh, what day is it
This October? And how many of them are there?

ABOVE DOOAGHTRY

Where the duach rises to a small plateau
That overlooks the sand dunes from Dooaghtry
To Roonkeel, and just beyond the cottage's
Higgledy perimeter fence-posts
At Carrigskeewaun, bury my ashes,

For the burial mound at Templedoomore
Has been erased by wind and sea, the same
Old stone-age sea that came as far inland
As Cloonaghmanagh and chose the place
That I choose as a promontory, a fort:

Let boulders at the top encircle me,
Neither a drystone wall nor a cairn, space
For the otter to die and the mountain hare
To lick snow stains from her underside,
A table for the peregrine and ravens,

A prickly double-bed as well, nettles
And carline-thistles, a sheeps' wool pillow,
So that, should she decide to join me there,
Our sandy dander to Allaran Point
Or Tonakeera will take for ever.

MARSH MARIGOLDS

in memory of Penny Cabot

Decades ago you showed me marsh marigolds
At Carrigskeewaun and behind a drystone wall
The waterlily lake's harvest of helleborines.

As you lie dying there can be only one lapwing
Immortalising at Dooaghtry your minty
Footsteps around the last of the yellow flags.

PETALWORT

for Michael Viney

You want your ashes to swirl along the strand
At Thallabaun – amongst clockwork, approachable,
Circumambulatory sanderlings, crab shells,
Bladderwrack, phosphorescence at spring tide –

Around the burial mound's wind-and-wave-inspired
Vanishing act – through dowel-holes in the wreck –
Into bottles but without a message, only
Self-effacement in sand, additional eddies.

There's no such place as heaven, so let it be
The Carricknashinnagh shoal or Caher
Island where you honeymooned in a tent
Amid the pilgrim-fishermen's stations,

Your spillet disentangling and trailing off
Into the night, a ghost on every hook – dab
And flounder, thorny skate – at ebb tide you
Kneeling on watery sand to haul them in.

Let us choose for the wreath a flower so small
Even you haven't spotted on the dune-slack
Between Claggan and Lackakeely its rosette –
Petalwort: snail snack, angel's nosegay.

CEILIDH

A ceilidh at Carrigskeewaun would now include
The ghost of Joe O'Toole at ease on his hummock
The far side of Corragaun Lake as he listens to
The O'Tooles from Inishdeigil who settled here
Eighty years ago, thirteen O'Tooles, each of them
A singer or fiddler, thirteen under the one roof,
A happy family but an unlucky one, Joe says,
And the visitors from Connemara who have rowed
Their currachs across the Killary for the music,
And my ghost at the duach's sheepbitten edge
Keeping an eye on the lamps in the windows here
But distracted by the nervy plover that pretends
A broken wing, by the long-lived oystercatcher
That calls out behind me from Thallabaun Strand.
The thirteen O'Tooles are singing about everything.
Their salty eggs are cherished for miles around.
There's a hazel copse near the lake without a name.
Dog violets, sorrel, wood spurge are growing there.
On Inishdeigil there's a well of the purest water.
Is that Arcturus or a faraway outhouse light?
The crescent moon's a coracle for Venus. Look.
Through the tide and over the Owennadornaun
Are shouldered the coffins of the thirteen O'Tooles.

AN OCTOBER SUN

in memory of Michael Hartnett

Something inconsolable in you looks me in the eye,
An October sun flashing off the rainy camber.
And something ironical too, as though we could
Warm our hands at turf stacks along the road.

Good poems are as comfortlessly constructed,
Each sod handled how many times. Michael, your
Poems endure the downpour like the skylark's
Chilly hallelujah, the robin's autumn song.

SHADOWS

I

A flat circle of flat stones, anonymous
Headstones commemorating the burial mound,
The dead suspended in the scenery
At head height roughly, unmoved by the wind:

Just as you and I swimming yesterday
At high tide beyond Allaran Point, now
Would be floundering in mid-air
Between that rock pool and the samphire ridge.

II

Seven hares encircle me and you
(We have counted them playing together)
Not too far from the hermitic snipe,

The otters we haven't seen for years
(Although today we heard one whistling)
Shadows between dragonfly and elver.

AFTER TRA-NA-ROSSAN

You were still far away. I was only the wind
When I wrote in my woolgathering twentieth
Year about an abstract expanse in Donegal:

'We walked on Tra-na-rossan strand;
the Atlantic winds were wiping the heat
from the August sun and the stretching sand
was cold beneath our naked feet;

our prints were washed and covered by the tide:
and so we walked through all our days
until there was too much to hide;
no wind to cool our open ways,

no passing tide to wash the traces
of transgression from the secret places.'

Then we filled the details in: a lapwing's
Reedy sigh above the duach, a tortoiseshell
Hilltopping on the cairn, autumn lady's tresses,
The sandwort-starry path to Carrigskeewaun.

I am looking at you through binoculars
As you open the galvanised aeolian gate
In silence and walk away towards the sea.

OVERHEAD

The beech tree looks circular from overhead
With its own little cumulus of exhalations.
Can you spot my skull under the nearby roof,
Its bald patch, the poem-cloud hanging there?

THE PATTERN

Thirty-six years, to the day, after our wedding
When a cold figure-revealing wind blew against you
And lifted your veil, I find in its fat envelope
The six-shilling *Vogue* pattern for your bride's dress,
Complicated instructions for stitching bodice
And skirt, box pleats and hems, tissue-paper outlines,
Semblances of skin which I nervously unfold
And hold up in snow light, for snow has been falling
On this windless day, and I glimpse your wedding dress
And white shoes outside in the transformed garden
Where the clothesline and every twig have been covered.

SNOW GEESE

So far away as to be almost absent
And yet so many of them we can hear
The line of snow geese along the horizon.
Tell me about cranberry fields, the harvest
Floating on flood water, acres of crimson.

I remember a solitary snow goose
Among smudgy cormorants on the Saltees
Decades ago. Today I calculate
Forty thousand snow geese, and pick for you
From the distance individual cranberries.

THE SETT

A friend's betrayal of you brings to mind
His anecdote about neighbours in Donegal
Who poured petrol into a badger's sett, that
Underground intelligence not unlike your own
Curling up among the root systems.
                                        Oh, why
Can the badger not have more than one address
Like the otter its hovers at Cloonaghmanagh
And Claggan and Carrigskeewaun, its holt
A glimmering between us at Dooaghtry?
I safeguard a bubble-rosary under ice.

ASCHY

We are both in our sixties now, our bodies
Growing stranger and more vulnerable.
It is time for that tonic called *aschy*,
Shadowy cherry-juice from South Russia.

The Argippaei who are all bald from birth,
Snub-nosed and long-chinned, lap it up
With lipsmacking gusto or mix it with milk
Or make pancakes out of the sediment.

In bitter spells they wrap the trunks with felt
As thick and white as the snowy weather.
A weird sanctity protects you and me
While we stay under our ponticum-tree.

STONECHAT

A flicker on the highest twig, a breast
That kindles the last of the fuchsia flowers
And the October sunset still to come
When we face the Carricknashinnagh shoal
And all the islands in a golden backwash
Where sanderlings scurry, two cormorants
Peeking at me and you over breakers
That interrupt the glow, behind us
A rainbow ascending out of Roonkeel
High above Six Noggins, disappearing
Between Mweelrea's crests, and we return
To the white cottage with its fuchsia hedge
To share for a second time the stonechat's
Flirtatious tail and flinty scolding.

DIPPER

Our only dipper on the Owennadornaun
Delayed us, so that we made it and no more
Through the spring tide, wading up to our waists:
Naked from the navel down, did we appear
Harmless to the golden plovers slow to rise
From their feeding on the waterlogged duach?
Then fire-gazing-and-log-and-turf-arranging
Therapy which should have unfrozen lust but
In the dark flood water a darker knot became
Two heron-unsettling-and-lapwing-lifting
Otters, our first for years at Carrigskeewaun,
And we rationed out binocular moments
Behind the curtains of the bedroom window
And watched them as they unravelled out of view.

ROBIN

A robin is singing from the cottage chimney.
Departure means stepping through the sound-drapes
Of his pessimistic skin-and-bone aubade.
Household chores begin: wiping wet windows
For Venus in greeny solitariness, sky-coin,
Morning's retina; scattering from the wonky
Bucket immaterial ashes over moor grass
Turned suddenly redder at the equinox;
Spreading newspapers by the hearth for blackened
Hailstones. We have slept next to the whoopers'
Nightlong echoing domestic hubbub.
A watery sun-glare is melting them.
His shadow on the lawn betrays the robin.
I would count the swans but it hurts my eyes.

SNIPE

in memory of Sheila Smyth

I wanted it to be a snipe from Belfast Lough's
Mud flats, the nightflier that juked into my headlights.
It could as well have been a knot or a godwit
From the Arctic, a bar-tailed godwit would you say?
Oh, what amateur ornithologists we are!
I had been out celebrating your life, and now
Here you were flapping into your immortality.
Everyone who loved you remembers how birdlike
Your body and behaviour were, exquisiteness.
I stopped the car and held in my lights the lost bird.
It froze like an illustration, the sensitive
Long beak disinclined to probe the tarmacadam.

WHEATEAR

Poem Beginning with a Line of J. M. Synge

Brown lark beside the sun
Supervising Carrigskeewaun
In late May, marsh marigolds
And yellow flags, trout at the low
Bridge hesitating, even
The ravens' ramshackle nest –
Applaud yourself, applaud me
As I find inside the cottage
A wheatear from Africa
Banging against the windowpane
And hold in my hands her creamy–
Buff underparts and white rump
And carry her to the door
And she joins you beside the sun
Before skimming across the dunes
To mimic in a rabbit hole
Among silverweed and speedwell
My panic, my breathlessness.

TWO PHEASANTS

As though from a catastrophic wedding reception
The cock pheasant in his elaborate waistcoat
Exploded over cultivated ground to where
A car in front of our car had crushed his bride.

I got the picture in no time in my wing-mirror
As in a woodcut by Hokusai who highlighted
The head for me, the white neck-ring and red wattles,
The long coppery tail, the elegance and pain.

HOUSE SPARROWS

The sparrows have quit our house, house sparrows
That cheeped in the gutters, stone-age hangers-on
That splashed in our puddles, dust-bathers.
                                        'Yea,
The sparrow hath found her an house.' But where?

Carthorses are munching oats from their nosebags
At a water trough surrounded by sparrows
That bicker and pick up the falling grains.

YELLOW BUNGALOW

after Gerard Dillon

A reproduction of your *Yellow Bungalow*
Hangs in our newfangled kitchen, dream-mirror,
A woman waiting between turf-box and window
For a young man to put away his accordion
And gut five anonymous fish for supper.

She appreciates the disposition of skillet
And kettle on the stovetop, of poker and tongs,
And keeps her distance in her faraway corner
Beside the Atlantic, while he has learned new tunes
And wants to accompany us to another room.

As soon as I've switched the fan-assisted oven on
And opened the bombinating refrigerator
(I've a meal to prepare) I hear bellows wheeze
And fingernails clitter over buttons and keys.
Cooking smells become part of the composition.

PRIMARY COLOURS

When Sarah went out painting in the wind,
A gust blew the palette from her hand
And splattered with primary colours
The footprints of wild animals.

She carried home *Low Cloud on Mweelrea*
And *Storm over Lackakeely*, leaving
Burnt Umber behind for the mountain hare
And for the otter Ultramarine.

DUSK

Poem Beginning with a Line of Ian Hamilton Finlay

Dusk is in the shed
and in the stable
now Rusty has gone
and her glossy knees
that smell of apple
or woodruff have gone
and her blaze has gone.

LOST

my lost lamb lovelier than all the wool

THE LAST FIELD

We who have fought are friends now all the time,
So walk with me to the last field on the farm
Where orchids grow – pyramidal, I confirm –
Under the hawthorn hedge and across the path
From higher-than-head-high maize, a pink wreath
On the limey flat-earth plain of County Meath,
As unexpected as the deadly nightshade
And scarlet pimpernel that hid in maize seed,
Stowaways, outcasts, exquisite beside
The dark green practical uprightness of your crop
(Fodder for cows), then other plants to look up
Later in the flora, but not before we stop
One dragonfly in our memories like a rhyme,
A farm animal from here on, we confirm
Who have fought and are friends now all the time.

THREE BUTTERFLIES

for Fleur Adcock

Your sister in New Zealand held the telephone
Above your mother in her open coffin
For you to communicate. How many times
Did silence encircle the globe before
The peacock butterfly arrived in your room?
We all know what the butterfly represents.
I granted my own mother a cabbage-white.
On the Dooaghtry cairn which commemorates
God knows whom a tortoiseshell alighted
To sun itself. It had been wintering
In memory's outhouse and escaped the wren.

THE PEAR

for John Montague

Someone has left three oranges and a pear
On Baudelaire's grave. Orchard of headstones.
The pear dangles in memory as from a branch.
Or is it a symbol, a poetic windfall,
A lucky sign? You put it in your pocket.

We have betrayed each other, we agree.
Like Peter, I suggest, not like Judas – no.
I love it when you link your arm with mine.
You eat half the pear and hand the rest to me.
The dead poet forgives the thieves their hunger.

OLD POETS

for Anne Stevenson

Old poets regurgitate
Pellets of chewed-up paper
Packed with shrew tails, frog bones,
Beetle wings, wisdom.

OWL CASES

for Medbh McGuckian

Leaving breath-haze and fingerprints
All over the glass case that contains
Barn-and-steeple familiars, we
Pick out the owl that is all ears,
As though tuning in with its feathers
To the togetherness of our heads.

Let us absorb Bubo bubo's
Hare-splitting claws, and such dark eyes
Above that wavering hoot (you know
The one) which is the voice of God,
And the face shaped like a heart
Or the shriek from a hollow tree.

We overlook the snowy owl
Snowdrifting in its separate case
Where it hunts by day, whose yellow gaze
Follows around the museum
Me and you, my dear, owl-lovers,
Lovers of otherworldliness.

LEVEL PEGGING

for Michael Allen

I

After a whole day shore fishing off Allaran Point
And Tonakeera you brought back one mackerel
Which I cooked with reverence and mustard sauce.
At the stepping stones near the burial mound
I tickled a somnolent salmon to death for you.
We nabbed nothing at all with the butterfly net.

Hunters, gatherers, would-be retiarii
We succeeded at least in entangling ourselves.
When the red Canadian kite became invisible
In Donegal, we fastened the line to a bollard
And sat for hours and looked at people on the pier
Looking up at our sky-dot, fishing in the sky.

II

You were driving my Escort in the Mournes when –
Brake-failure – Robert Lowell and you careered
Downhill: 'Longley's car is a bundle of wounds.'
When his last big poem had done for Hugh MacDiarmid
And he collapsed, we wrapped his dentures in a hanky
And carried them like a relic to the hospital.

We looked after poets after a fashion. And you
Who over the decades in the Crown, the Eglantine,
The Bot, the Wellie, the Chelsea have washed down
Poetry and pottage without splashing a page
And scanned for life-threatening affectation
My latest 'wee poem' – you have looked after me.

III

I was a booby-trapped corpse in the squaddies' sights.
The arsehole of nowhere. Dawn in a mountainy bog.
From the back seat alcohol fumed as I slumbered
Surrounded by Paras, then – all innocence – you
Turned up with explanations and a petrol can.
They lowered their rifles when I opened my eyes.

Our Stingers-and-Harvey-Wallbangers period
With its plaintive anthem 'The Long and Winding Road'
Was a time of assassinations, tit-for-tat
Terror. You were Ulster's only floating voter, your
Political intelligence a wonky hedgehopping
Bi-plane that looped the loop above the killing fields.

IV

Rubbed out by winds Anaximines imagined,
The burial mound at Templedoomore has gone.
Locals have driven their tractors along the strand
And tugged apart the wooden wreck for gateposts.
There are fewer exits than you'd think, fewer spars
For us to build our ship of death and sail away.

Remember playing cards to the crash of breakers,
Snipe drumming from the estuary, smoky gossip
In Carrigskeewaun about marriages and making wills?
I'll cut if you deal – a last game of cribbage, burnt
Matches our representatives, stick men who race
Slowly round the board with peg legs stuck in the hole.

TWO SKUNKS

Why, my dear octogenarian Jewish friend,
Does the menagerie of minuscule glass animals
On top of your tv set not include a skunk?
I have been travelling around in America,
Sleeping in wooden houses with squeaky floors,
Landings hung with pictures of lost relatives,
Professors, stationmasters, wise embroiderers.
Driving along the Delaware my poet-host
Stops to let two wild turkeys cross the road.
Is that a third one dithering behind us?
We wind the car windows up – a freshly
Flattened skunk so pongily alive in death
Even the magpies in the dogwood hesitate.
Later we laugh as a three-legged dachshund
Raises its non-existent limb to piddle
At the only set of traffic lights in town.
Laid out in its cotton-wool-lined golden box
A skunk in the Novelty Store beguiles me.
Dawnlight and birdsong kindle my fourposter.
I swaddle your present in my underclothes
For it is time to pack and leave America.
A cardinal flusters at the bedroom window
Like the soul of a little girl who hands over
All of the red things her short life recalls.
Here, my dear octogenarian Jewish friend,
Is my gift for you, a skunk spun out of glass
And so small as to be almost unbreakable.

EDWARD THOMAS'S POEM

I

I couldn't make out the minuscule handwriting
In the notebook the size of his palm and crinkled
Like an origami quim by shell-blast that stopped
His pocket watch at death. I couldn't read the poem.

II

From where he lay he could hear the skylark's
Skyward exultation, a chaffinch to his left
Fidgeting among the fallen branches,
Then all the birds of the Western Front.

III

The nature poet turned into a war poet as if
He could cure death with the rub of a dock leaf.

SYCAMORE

The sycamore stumps survived the deadliest gales
To put out new growth, leaves sticky with honeydew
And just enough white wood to make a violin.

This was a way of mending the phonograph record
Broken by the unknown soldier before the Somme
(Fritz Kreisler playing Dvořák's 'Humoresque').

The notes of music twirled like sycamore wings
From farmhouse-sheltering-and-dairy-cooling branches
And carried to all corners of the battlefield.

THE PAINTERS

John Lavery rescued self-heal from waste ground
At Sailly-Sallisel in nineteen-seventeen, and framed
One oblong flower-head packed with purple flowers
Shaped like hooks, a survivor from the battlefield.

When I shouldered my father's coffin his body
Shifted slyly and farted and joined up again
With rotting corpses, old pals from the trenches.
William Orpen said you couldn't paint the smell.

PIPISTRELLE

They kept him alive for years in warm water,
The soldier who had lost his skin.
                                    At night
He was visited by the wounded bat
He had unfrozen after Passchendaele,

Locking its heels under his forefinger
And whispering into the mousy fur.

Before letting the pipistrelle flicker
Above his summery pool and tipple there,

He spread the wing-hand, elbow to thumb.
The membrane felt like a poppy petal.

HARMONICA

A tommy drops his harmonica in No Man's Land.
My dad like old Anaximines breathes in and out
Through the holes and reeds and finds this melody.

Our souls are air. They hold us together. Listen.
A music-hall favourite lasts until the end of time.
My dad is playing it. His breath contains the world.

The wind is playing an orchestra of harmonicas.

THE FRONT

I dreamed I was marching up to the Front to die.
There were thousands of us who were going to die.
From the opposite direction, out of step, breathless,
The dead and wounded came, all younger than my son,
Among them my father who might have been my son.
'What is it like?' I shouted after the family face.
'It's cushy, mate! Cushy!' my father-son replied.

PINE MARTEN

That stuffed pine marten in the hotel corridor
Ended up on all fours in nineteen-thirteen
And now is making it across No Man's Land where
A patrol of gamekeepers keeps missing him.

WAR & PEACE

Achilles hunts down Hector like a sparrowhawk
Screeching after a horror-struck collared-dove
That flails just in front of her executioner, so
Hector strains under the walls of Troy to stay alive.
Past the windbent wild fig tree and the lookout
Post they both accelerate away from the town
Along a cart-track as far as double well-heads
That gush into the eddying Scamander, in one
Warm water steaming like smoke from a bonfire,
The other running cold as hailstones, snow water,
Handy for the laundry-cisterns carved out of stone
Where Trojan housewives and their pretty daughters
Used to rinse glistening clothes in the good old days,
On washdays before the Greek soldiers came to Troy.

INTERVIEW

'No one has ever lived a luckier life than you,
Achilles, nor ever will: when you were alive
We looked up to you as one of the gods, and now
As a resident down here you dominate the dead.'

'Not even you can make me love death, Odysseus:
I'd far rather clean out ditches on starvation
Wages for some nonentity of a smallholder
Than lord it over the debilitated dead.'

SLEEP & DEATH

Zeus the cloud-gatherer said to sunny Apollo:
'Sponge the congealed blood from Sarpedon's corpse,
Take him far away from here, out of the line of fire,
Wash him properly in a stream, in running water,
And rub supernatural preservative over him
And wrap him up in imperishable fabrics,
Then hand him over to those speedy chaperons,
Sleep and his twin brother Death, who will bring him
In no time at all to Lycia's abundant farmland
Where his family will bury him with grave-mound
And grave-stone, the entitlement of the dead.'
And Apollo did exactly as he was told:
He carried Sarpedon out of the line of fire,
Washed him properly in a stream, in running water,
And rubbed supernatural preservative over him
And wrapped him up in imperishable fabrics
And handed him over to the speedy chaperons,
Sleep and his twin brother Death, who brought him
In no time at all to Lycia's abundant farmland.

THE MINER

How many of my relatives worked down the mine?
The page of William Longley of Ryhope Colliery
In the Durham Miners' Book of Remembrance
Coincides with my short visit to the cathedral.
Let him who 'breaketh open a shaft' rub shoulders
With the carpenters and blacksmiths and wood-reeves
And gamekeepers and horsehair-curlers whose names
And professions and parentheses I know about
Because they influenced my self-centred make-up
And lived and worked in this other country long ago.
When they turn the page tomorrow, William Longley
Will disappear back into darkness and danger
And crawl on hands and knees in the crypt of the world
Under houses and outhouses and workshops and fields.

IN NOTRE-DAME

When I go back into the cathedral to check
If the candle I lit for you is still burning,
I encounter Job squatting on his dunghill
(Can those be cowrie-shell fossils in the stone?
No. Imagine imagining and carving turds
At eye-level for our sorry edification!).
Such tiny figures make my own body feel huge
And fleshy and hopeless inside the doorway.
In my voice-box the penitents and pickpockets
Murmuring in hundreds down the aisles find room.
Each mouth is a cathedral for the God-crumbs.
Where is the holy water, the snow water for Job?
All of our eyes are broken rose windows.
Your candle singes the eyelashes of morning.

A NORWEGIAN WEDDING

Because the Leprosy Museum is still closed
We find ourselves in St Olaf's, eavesdropping
On a Norwegian wedding. The Lutheran light
Picks us out from among the small congregation.
How few friends anyone has. I'm glad we came.
Christ holds his hands up high above the lovers
And fits his death into the narrow window. Oh,
His sore hands. How many friends does a leper have?
Bride and bridegroom walk past us and into the rain.
It is mid-May. All of the roads out of Bergen
Are bordered with lady's smock and wood anemones.

MONTALE'S DOVE

He writes about a dove that flies away from him
Between the pillars of Ely Cathedral – wing
Clatter and aphrodisiac burbling as well as
Sepulchral knick-knack – a lover's soul escaping.

After a life-time of honey-coloured sunlight
He craves darkness – not death exactly but a nest
Perhaps, a hole in the religious masonry
For resurrection under a smouldering breast.

He doesn't mention how the stained-glass windows
Make walls a momentary rainbow patchwork if
The sun is shining: instead he lets one white feather
Drift among terrible faces up in the roof.

UP THERE

after Giovanni Pascoli

The skylark far away up there in dawnlight
Sky-wanders: arias fall on the farmhouse
While smoke sways raggedly this way and that.

Far away up there the tiny eye takes in
Furrows rolling over in brown munificence
Behind converging teams of white oxen.

A particular sod on black soggy land
Flashes in sunlight like a mirror fragment:
The philosophical labourer binding sheaves
Cocks an ear for the cuckoo's recitatives.

THE LIZARD

At the last restaurant on the road to Pisa airport
The only thing under the pergola to distract me
From the gnocchi stuffed with walnuts in porcini sauce
Was a greeny lizard curving her belly like a bowl
So that when she tucked her hind legs behind her
In philosophical fashion and lifted up her hands
As though at prayer or in heated *conversazione,*
She wouldn't scorch her elegant fingers or toes
On the baking concrete and would feel the noon
As no more than a hot buckle securing her eggs.
We left the restaurant on the road to Pisa airport
And flew between Mont Blanc and the Matterhorn.
His lady co-pilot, the captain of our Boeing
Coyly let us know, specialised in smooth landings.

WOODEN HARE

Sarah drew a hare under a sky full of large stars
When she was ten: now, more than a childhood later,
In antique Paraty where the sea seeps up the street
Depositing between boulder-sized cobbles sand
And the feathers of snowy egrets and frigate birds,
We meet the hare again, an 'indigenous artefact',
And want to know everything about the animal,
Its crouching body carved out of caxeto, ears
Slotted into the skull, the unexpected markings
(Blotches of butum oil) that represent leaf-shadows
Or are they stars fallen through the forest canopy?
Dare we buy it and bring it back home to Ireland,
The hare in Sarah's picture, the Mato Grosso hare?
Its eyes are made from beeswax and mother-of-pearl.

IRISH HARE

Amid São Paulo's endless higgledy concrete
I found in a dream your form again, but woven
Out of banana leaf and Brazilian silence
By the Wayana Indians, as though to last.

TAXONOMY

Poets used to measure with a half-crown baby toads
Just this size, and bring to life their vague muck-colour.
Ten years ago I counted glow-worms at the waterfall.
Into the puddle that was the salamander's pool
A dragonfly inserts her long bum and lays eggs.
I have fitted a hundred wing-glints into this one line.

EARTHSHINE

The Indian boy has blackened his face
As though to imitate the sun's eclipse
Or the moon's, or the forest's shadowiness:
For me he means earthshine, earthlight
Faintly illuminating the crescent moon's
Unsunlit surface: his lips and his eyes
Are watery glimmers and his headdress
An irradiation of white heron feathers.

WOODSMOKE

for Helen Denerley

I

I have just arrived and hesitate between
Water-sounds and your metallic menagerie.
I am lost among the pheasants' heather stands.
A kestrel stoops as though you put him there
With the buzzards high on their thermals criss-
Crossing. Translations, Helen, metaphors.
The mare and stag you made from scrap metal
Are moving in slow motion across your land.
You filled the mare with air and the millennium.
The stag that flashes antlers and pizzle
Was conceived once you spotted in your heap
A tongue for him, a cobbler's last: his tail
Is another cobbler's last. Clashnettie means
(You think) the hollow of the juniper tree.

II

Among the pourers of the molten iron
Were the threatened and bereaved, disguised
In helmets and leather aprons, balancing
Buckets of terror as the furnace roared.
The Deskry's meander does not require
An iron bridge: you and your friends put up
A black rainbow, a darkbow to reflect
The moonbow that shone the January night
A neighbour's two boys were burnt alive,
A whitebow of snow and frost and moonlight
Supporting your cast-iron fourteen-foot span
Across the shallow water, snow water,
From soggy pasture to where the rainbow ends,
Just there, among ragged robin and harebells.

III

You wanted the kiln to look like a cairn,
A hikers' and lovers' accumulation,
But inside is a clay-lined, bottle-shaped
Emptiness, a hole for the rainwater
And our pebbles. Can you hear them falling?
Whereabouts in your workshop at Clashnettie
Are the leather aprons and gaiters, the boots
With steel toecaps that glint in the moonlight?
Fire splashing over into Deskry Water
Made pocketfuls of accidental sculpture
For children from the glen. Smoke and steam.
You have left a scrap-iron golden eagle
On a boulder up the slopes of Morven
Where he rests in gales near a picnic hut.

IV

You pictured a heron feeding her mate
Or sipping at her own reflection, two
Heads, the bridge's arc, rainbow's template.
It took ten tappings from the sparky kiln.
I picture a heron beneath the bridge
Or, where the boys lie buried, a motionless
Graveside sentinel waiting for ever
To regurgitate field-mouse and water-vole.
What bits and pieces would make a heron?
You put to use for the golden eagle's wings
Tines from a harrow so rusted away
A horse drew it once, or the first tractor.
I am looking for a heron's feather,
A crown-feather preferably, a black one.

V

You take me to someone else's barbecue,
Strangers gazing at a bonfire, catherine
Wheels and roman candles among the pines
And, as though I am remembering it,
The scent of woodruff under woodsmoke.
Are there people here who are not your friends?
A mother who doesn't understand, a sister?
I am with you. From among the shadowy
Mystifying voices I pick out yours.
We have to imagine one another
Quickly, and then go home, I to the town,
Clothes reeking of smoke and uneasiness,
You to your acre, the dark plantation,
The stream, the dipper bobbing on his stone.

HELEN'S MONKEY

You saw the exhaust and inlet ports as ears,
The hole for measuring Top Dead Centre
(Piston-timing) as a nose, making the eyes
Valve-inspection covers (no longer there).
It took time, Helen, for the monkey's skull
(The cylinder head from a twenties Blackburn)
To find a body: it sat on the windowsill
Through a long evolutionary autumn
Until you came across the unimaginable –
The frame of a motorbike (and a side-car's)
Hidden by snow and heather up a hill
Near Ullapool, a twenties Blackburn of course,
Skeleton recognising skull, and soul
A monkey's soul amalgamated with yours.

PRAXILLA

Sunlight strews leaf-shadows on the kitchen floor.
Is it the beech tree or the basil plant or both?
Praxilla was *not* 'feeble-minded' to have Adonis
Answer that questionnaire in the underworld:
'Sunlight's the most beautiful thing I leave behind,
Then the shimmering stars and the moon's face,
Also ripe cucumbers and apples and pears.'
She is helping me unpack these plastic bags.
I subsist on fragments and improvisations.
Lysippus made a bronze statue of Praxilla
Who 'said nothing worthwhile in her poetry'
And set her groceries alongside the sun and moon.

CORINNA

Have you fallen asleep for ever, Corinna?
In the past you were never the one to lie in.

THE GROUP

I

With Ion of Chios, the prize-winning poet
Who specialises in astronomical phenomena
And the invention of compound adjectives,
I hang around for the sun's white-winged
Forerunner, the air-wandering dawn-star
(And for the splashing-out of good wine).

II

Lamprocles, the dithyrambic poet,
Says the ethereal Pleiades share
The same nomenclature as wood-pigeons.
I must ask him what he makes of that.

III

Myrtis, lyrical poetess from Anthedon,
Craftswoman of a few immortal lines
(A voice like a skylark on a good day)
Overdoes things a bit and goes in for
The same poetry competition as Pindar.

IV

Hypochondriacal Telesilla
For the sake of her health takes up singing
And playing the lyre and gets well enough
To volunteer and man the battlements,
Female defeating male and inspiring
Argos, her hometown, with poetry.

V

Devoutly we coldshoulder Diagoras
For blowing the whistle (in poem and dance)
On the Eleusinian Mysteries: also,
There's a talent of silver for his killer.

VI

A certain person boozes and gorges
And says scandalous things about us all,
Punching the air, 'I've plenty of blows left
If anyone wants to take me on,' he bawls.
The Group would be far better off without
Timocreon of Rhodes (poet, pentathlete).

VII

Oblivious to being out of date,
Which of us will not appear as dopey
As Charixenna, oldfashioned pipe-player
And composer of oldfashioned tunes
And, according to some, a poet too?

WHITE WATER

in memory of James Simmons

Jimmy, you isolated yourself
At the last bend before white water.
We should have been fat jolly poets
In some oriental print who float
Cups of warm saké to one another
On the river, and launch in paper boats
Their poems. We are all separated.
Your abandoned bivouac should be called
Something like the Orchid Pavilion.

HERON

in memory of Kenneth Koch

You died the day I was driving to Carrigskeewaun
(A remote townland in County Mayo, I explain,
Meaning, so far as I know, The Rock of the Wall Fern)
And although it was the wettest Irish year I got the car
Across the river and through the tide with groceries
And laundry for my fortnight among the waterbirds.
If I'd known you were dying, Kenneth, I'd have packed
Into cardboard boxes all your plays and poems as well
And added to curlew and lapwing anxiety-calls
The lyric intensity of your New York Jewish laughter.
You would have loved the sandy drive over the duach
('The what?'), over the machair ('the what?'), the drive
Through the white gateposts and the galvanised gate
Tied with red string, the starlings' sleeping quarters,
The drive towards turf-fired hilarity and disbelief,
'Where are all those otters, Longley, and all those hares?
I see only sparrows here and house sparrows at that!'
You are so tall and skinny I shall conscript a heron
To watch over you on hang-glider wings, old soldier,
An ashy heron, *ardea cinerea,* I remind you
(A pedant neither smallminded nor halfhearted):
'And *cinerarius?*': a slave who heats the iron tongs
In hot ashes for the hair-dresser, a hair-curler
Who will look after every hair on your curly head.
That afternoon was your night-season. I didn't know.
I didn't know that you were 'poured out like water
And all your bones were out of joint'. I didn't know.
Tuck your head in like a heron and trail behind you
Your long legs, take to the air above a townland
That encloses Carrigskeewaun and Central Park.

LEAVES

Is this my final phase? Some of the poems depend
Peaceably like the brown leaves on a sheltered branch.
Others are hanging on through the equinoctial gales
To catch the westering sun's red declension.
I'm thinking of the huge beech tree in our garden.
I can imagine foliage on fire like that.

X

TWO NEW POEMS

THE LEVERET

for my grandson, Benjamin

This is your first night in Carrigskeewaun.
The Owennadornaun is so full of rain
You arrived in Paddy Morrison's tractor,
A bumpy approach in your father's arms
To the cottage where, all of one year ago,
You were conceived, a fire-seed in the hearth.
Did you hear the wind in the fluffy chimney?
Do you hear the wind tonight, and the rain
And a shore bird calling from the mussel reefs?
Tomorrow I'll introduce you to the sea,
Little hoplite. Have you been missing it?
I'll park your chariot by the otters' rock
And carry you over seaweed to the sea.
There's a tufted duck on David's lake
With her sootfall of hatchlings, pompoms
A day old and already learning to dive.
We may meet the stoat near the erratic
Boulder, a shrew in his mouth, or the merlin
Meadow-pipit-hunting. But don't be afraid.
The leveret breakfasts under the fuchsia
Every morning, and we shall be watching.
I have picked wild flowers for you, scabious
And centaury in a jam-jar of water
That will bend and magnify the daylight.
This is your first night in Carrigskeewaun.

THE WREN

I am writing too much about Carrigskeewaun,
I think, until you two come along, my grandsons,
And we generalise at once about cows and sheep.
A day here represents a life-time, bird's-foot trefoil
Among wild thyme, dawn and dusk muddled on the ground,
The crescent moon fading above Mweelrea's shoulder
As hares sip brackish water at the stepping stones
And the innovative raven flips upside down
As though for you.
               I burble under your siesta
Like a contrapuntal runnel, and the heather
Stand that shelters the lesser twayblade shelters you.
We sleepwalk around a townland whooper swans
From the tundra remember, and the Saharan
Wheatear. I want you both to remember me
And what the wind-tousled wren has been saying
All day long from fence posts and the fuchsia depths,
A brain-rattling bramble-song inside a knothole.

INDEX OF TITLES

INDEX OF FIRST LINES

She stood among the nasturtiums on a rubbish dump, 204
Since the day after he was conceived his father, 180
Since you, Mind, think to diagnose, 11
Snow curls into the coalhouse, flecks the coal, 126
Snow piles up against the sunny window, 235
So far away as to be almost absent, 294
Someone has left three oranges and a pear, 302
Some people tried to stop other people wearing poppies, 226
Something inconsolable in you looks me in the eye, 292
Sometimes the quilts were white for weddings, the design, 269
Sometimes you and I are like rope-makers, 45
So much is implied on that furthest strand, 34
So small its brassy hand, 218
So white are the white flowers in the white garden that I, 234
Stained with blood from a hare, 96
Standing behind the god Poseidon I can see, 220
Stand me a last one for the road ahead, 162
Stepping among recent windfalls and couch grass, 247
Still looking for a scoothole, Phemios the poet, 229
Sunlight strews leaf-shadows on the kitchen floor, 320
Sydney our mutual friend is kneeling by your bed, 263

That could be me lying there, 80
That stuffed pine marten in the hotel corridor, 309
That time I tagged along with my dad to the dry cleaners, 221
The artist in my father transformed the diagonal, 273
The beech tree looks circular from overhead, 293
The brightest star came out, the day star, dawn's star, 171
The cries of the shipwrecked enter my head, 18
The day we buried your two years and two months, 263
The doddery English veterans are getting, 224
The dying fall, the death spasm, 41
The exhausted cathedral reaches nowhere near the sky, 256
The freeze-up annexes the sea even, 19
The ghosts of the aunt and uncles I never knew, 176
The headstone for my parents' grave in Drumbo churchyard, 232
The Hebridean gales mere sycophants, 36
The Indian boy who has blackened his face, 316
The length of white silk I selected, 209
The little rowing boat was full of, 84
The lodger is writing a novel, 83
The markings almost disappear, 156
The moment I heard that Oisín Ferran had died in a fire, 231
The moon beams like Eva Braun's bare bottom, 186
The moustache Edward Thomas grew to cover up, 258
The oars, heavy with seaweed, at rest in humid mists, 211

Unmarked were the bodies of the soldier-poets, 136
Unweatherbeaten as the moon my face, 19

Water through the window, the light and shade, 26
We are both in our sixties now, our bodies, 295
We crossed the fields by moonlight and by moonlight, 244
We listen for quails among ferns and twigs, 175
We postmodernists can live with that human head, 199
We returned to the empty ballroom, 85
We should have been galloping on horses, their hoofprints, 243
We've put a necklace on the naked wood, a crown, 181
We who have fought are friends now all the time, 304
We would follow that New Orleans marching band, 173
What class of a nightmare are you living through, 252
What does the sandpiper know of the river changing course, 239
What they are doing makes their garden feel like a big room, 217
When a single sheet's too heavy and the night perspires, 174
When he described how he had built the ingenious bedroom, 177
When he found Laertes alone on the tidy terrace, hoeing, 182
When he had made sure there were no survivors in his house, 194
When he lays out as on a market stall or altar, 204
When Helen, destroyer of cities, destroyer of men, 251
When he was billeted in a ruined house in Arras, 255
When in good time corpses go off and ooze in the heat, 202
When I go back into the cathedral to check, 312
When I told you on the day my mother died, 185
When I was left alone with our first-born, 250
When I was young I wrote that flowers are very slow flames, 217
When millions march into the mincing machine, 255
When my father stumbled over gassy corpses, 223
When my fingers touch your body's, 154
When Nausicaa described to Odysseus how her mother, 283
When Sarah went out painting in the wind, 300
When shiny Hector reached out for his son, the wean, 226
When someone's afflicted with the itchy nirls, 200
When sweeties came back to Mrs Parker's shop we, 262
When the swallow detoured into the kitchen, 176
When they cut off his head, the long whiskers, 116
When those who had eaten at our table and drunk, 270
When you weighed against, 172
When you woke me up and showed me through the window, 182
'Where am I?' Consulting the *Modern School Atlas*, 233
Where the burn separating Carrigskeewaun, 276
Where the duach rises to a small plateau, 289
Where there's nothing to fell but hazel scrub and hawthorn, 169
While I was looking for Easter snow on the hills, 253

There's a dip in the mattress where I sleep.
Rise out of your hollow hours before me
Every morning, and on the last morning
Tuck me in behind our windbreak of books.